HOW TO THINK CRITICALLY

HOW TO THINK CRITICALLY

A CONCISE GUIDE

Jeff McLaughlin

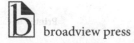

broadview press

LIBRARY AND ARCHIVES CANADA CATALOGUING IN PUBLICATION

McLaughlin, Jeff, 1962-, author
    How to think critically : a concise guide / Jeff McLaughlin.

Includes index.
ISBN 978-1-55481-216-5 (pbk.)

    1. Critical thinking—Textbooks. 2. Logic—Textbooks. I. Title.

BC177.M25 2014   160   C2014-902855-5

BROADVIEW PRESS is an independent, international publishing house, incorporated in 1985.

We welcome comments and suggestions regarding any aspect of our publications—please feel free to contact us at the addresses below or at broadview@broadviewpress.com.

NORTH AMERICA
Post Office Box 1243
Peterborough, Ontario
K9J 7H5 Canada

555 Riverwalk Parkway
Tonawanda, NY 14150, USA
TEL: (705) 743–8990
FAX: (705) 743–8353

customerservice@broadviewpress.com

UK, EUROPE, CENTRAL ASIA, MIDDLE EAST, AFRICA, INDIA, AND SOUTHEAST ASIA
Eurospan Group, 3 Henrietta St., London WC2E 8LU, United Kingdom
tel: 44 (0) 1767 604972 fax: 44 (0) 1767 601640
eurospan@turpin-distribution.com

AUSTRALIA AND NEW ZEALAND
NewSouth Books
c/o TL Distribution, 15–23 Helles Ave.
Moorebank, NSW 2170, Australia
tel: (02) 8778 9999 fax: (02) 8778 9944
orders@tldistribution.com.au

www.broadviewpress.com

Broadview Press acknowledges the financial support of the Government of Canada through the Canada Book Fund for our publishing activities.

Edited by Betsy Struthers
Typesetting by Em Dash Design

Printed in Canada

This one is for my sister Marni

Early on in my university teaching career, Marni came to visit me. She sat in the back of the lecture hall while I was explaining Venn diagrams to the students (see Chapter 7). Afterwards, she said to me, "So, it's like this, right?" and went on to show me that she had grasped the concepts immediately.

That act also reassured me and made me feel good about what I was doing and how I was doing it—something my sister does all the time for everyone around her.

Contents

PART II: THE SCIENCE OF CRITICAL THINKING

Preface

Dear Reader,

This work is based on over 20 years of teaching critical thinking and is part of my attempt to make learning the topic less intimidating but still scholastically rigorous. I hope you find it useful for your everyday life as well as your academic studies.

This book was in part supported by a sabbatical leave from Thompson Rivers University; during that time, I was in a serious motor vehicle accident in Graz, Austria. So the first example in Chapter 1 now strikes me as a bit ironic. Had I been more careful in my own reasoning, I might not have been hit. (You'll see what I mean when you read the example.) I am grateful for the love and support of my dear family and friends who came together to help me get through the long and often extremely painful healing process. Interestingly, it also gave me a good opportunity to directly experience the Austrian health care system, which gave me stories to use for my medical ethics course.

With so many broken ribs, I couldn't give them the hugs that I wanted or needed at the time. So now I'm catching up and sending out big hugs to my sister Marni McLaughlin, my ex-wife Deanna Balderson, Kathi Bantleon, Heinz Auernig, Walter Scholger, and Adel Awad. There were so many people—including Chris Alpassy-Pastirk, Joseph "Peppi" Grohs, Roman Höller, Stefan Körösi, Kasia Krakowczyk, Nick Martin, Dieter Schicker, Manfred "Speedy" Temmel, and Veronika Wolf—who expressed sincere concern and wanted to help that it was (and remains) overwhelming. One cannot (by definition) expect the unexpected—be it good or bad. Fortunately, because of all of those who surrounded me with love, I found much good in what was a terrible situation.

I am also indebted to my other colleagues at Karl-Franzens-Universität, including Dr. Johannes Stigler, Martina Semlak, and Gunter Vasold.

I am grateful to all the reviewers of my manuscript for their time, helpful insight, and kind words.

Finally, I want to express my thanks to Broadview Press. The team, headed up by Stephen Latta, was a joy to work with and any editorial suggestions they had only made this book better.

Jeff McLaughlin

This book has a companion website with interactive review materials, additional examples, and other features. If you purchased a used copy of this book and wish to use the companion website, please visit <www.broadviewpress.com> to purchase a code.

PART I

THE ART OF CRITICAL THINKING

CHAPTER 1
Identifying Arguments and Non-Arguments

1.1 Introduction

Critical thinking involves the assessment and evaluation of arguments—not just the kind of arguments you encounter in philosophy but the kind you come across every day. You need good reasoning skills in order to successfully reflect upon and respond to political commentary, newspaper reports, and mass media advertising. Confidence with these skills will help you discuss potentially lively issues in class, in the workplace, and even at the dinner table.

If you are able to identify and understand the arguments of others, and if you can analyze and evaluate these arguments to distinguish the good ones from the bad ones, and if you can construct your own arguments and defend them, then you'll have a powerful tool to assist you in doing whatever you do in your life. Accordingly, the appropriate readership for this little book of critical thinking is vast—ranging from first-year students at college and university to anyone who needs to learn how to carefully assess the views of others while defending his or her own beliefs.

This book is divided into two parts. The first six chapters may be grouped under a heading called the "art of critical thinking," as they look at how best to use language to construct successful arguments for everyday reasoning. The second part, which consists of Chapters 7 and 8, may be called the "science of critical thinking," since these chapters provide steadfast and exacting rules (much like mathematics) that reveal how precisely the bits and pieces of logic and language fit together.

While much of what is here may be new to you—especially the terminology—it is perhaps more appropriate to refer to this book as a *re-introduction* to critical thinking. This is because you are already thinking critically, and you've been doing it for quite some time whether you realize it or not. You need to critically reflect upon and think about what to believe in order to survive each and every day. This book will show you how to further develop and refine this capacity that you possess.

Tempted to cross the street but there's a car coming? You're engaged in critical thinking. Considering leaving for school later than you did yesterday? You will be engaged in critical thinking. Trying to figure out what to eat for dinner tonight? That's critical thinking. Wondering what to wear today given the gloomy weather forecast? Ditto. Even deciding to buy this book involved some degree of critical thinking. What is common in all of these examples is that you are making a decision and drawing a conclusion about what to do or what to think based upon various bits of evidence or prior knowledge or judgements. In other words, you formed an argument and acted from it.

Consider that at some point in your life someone taught you to look both ways to make sure that there were no cars coming before you crossed the road. Now that you're an adult, you might be more of a risk-taker (or a faster runner) and decide that you can beat the oncoming vehicle. Whether you stay or go, you're still making a decision based upon your past experience and knowledge. You think and judge quickly: you go from surveying what is going on around you to recognizing that there's a car approaching. You draw upon a generalization from years of previous road crossings and combine it with an assessment regarding how much risk you are currently willing to take along with whatever you know about the way things work in the world (e.g., what a massive piece of moving metal can do to the human body).

Suppose you go home tonight, open up your refrigerator, and see a sample of one of your favourite foods. You're hungry so you choose to eat it because you know that it will satisfy your hunger. You're thinking critically. Now imagine that you see that the food seems to have an unnatural neon sheen that wasn't there last month and an odour unlike anything you've smelled before. Now you choose not to eat it. Again, you're thinking critically.

Finally, consider why you chose to read this text. You may have a number of grounds for doing so—some that might be considered good and others that might be considered bad. Perhaps it is required for your class; perhaps it sounded useful; perhaps you wanted to impress your colleagues by showing them the types of books you like to read at the beach for fun. Whatever the reasons, you acted upon them, and here you are reading these very words. You chose on the basis of one or more reasons to get this book. You rationally moved from a claim (whatever it might be—and it doesn't matter how silly it might seem right now) to a conclusion based upon that claim. In other words, you developed an argument and were thinking critically. Someone might be able to challenge the satisfactoriness of the reasons you put forward (e.g., if you try to read this book at the beach, you might fall asleep and get a nasty sunburn), but at least you have your reasons! When you do things or believe things without having *any* reasons (as opposed to having weak reasons), you are not thinking critically. You are just reacting without thought, judging without care.

Critical thinking is an important skill. Let's make that statement stronger: *Critical thinking is a necessary and essential skill.* At a minimum, it is a skill that forms the foundation of what you need for all your other interests. As a skill, it is something that needs to be practised and worked on in order to improve. Think about learning math. Can you learn how to do algebra just by reading a book? No, you have to try it for yourself. Can you learn to drive a car by just reading the student manual? If you think you can, please tell others when you are on the road so that they can get off it! Can you learn a foreign language without practice? Nein! Indeed, even the top athletes in the world must continually practise what they are best at.

Speaking of practice, there are many exercises here for you to try, both on your own and with a colleague. You will find answers to many of the questions in the Solutions to Chapter Exercises section. To start off, here is a fun test of your ability to present your thoughts to another person in a clear and logical fashion: try to think about all the steps that are involved in tying your shoes or putting on your jacket. Write them down and have a colleague follow your directions exactly. You'll soon find that even with something that you do every day, it takes a bit of work to get it right when explaining it properly to someone else.

For example, did you point out which shoe goes on which foot? Even if you know how to get it right, it is a challenge to get others to grasp what you mean as opposed to what you actually said or wrote (e.g., if you just wrote "Put on the jacket," your colleague might put it on backwards or put legs through the arms). Even if you know exactly what you mean, others will not understand you unless you lay out your meaning clearly and explicitly. This is especially the case in argumentation.

Some people don't think critically enough. They just accept without questioning, without exploring alternatives, without examining other options. However, just as Socrates told us that the unexamined life is not worth living, the unexamined argument is not worth accepting.

The purpose of this book is to show you how best to develop your critical thinking abilities so that you can succeed in presenting your point of view, improving it when and where necessary, and responding appropriately to people who disagree with you. In the end, you may find that the beliefs you now hold can rightly persuade others, or you may find that your own views need to be modified. Sometimes all that is required is a minor adjustment, but other times you may be convinced by others that what you once thought was right really isn't right after all.

1.2 Arguments, Not Fights

Cross the street; eat the food; take this course; vote for that person; support a worthy cause; defend an unpopular view. Critical thinking requires that you understand, analyze, and evaluate arguments (your own and those of others) in accordance with certain rules of rational thought. *To think critically doesn't mean just to be negative and criticize but to assess and evaluate reasons and then draw the appropriate conclusion.*

By **argument** we don't mean the yelling and screaming and breaking of expensive dishes variety of quarrels. Nor do we mean the name-calling and hurt feelings variety either. Instead, we mean something more like an examination of ideas and beliefs. When you argue, you are providing reasons as to why one should accept or reject a claim. An argument can be made for your own benefit—when you are deciding what to think or do—or for the persuasion of others.

In constructing arguments, you'll be compiling a series of claims that consist of reasons—which are technically referred to as **premises**—that (ideally) establish a belief, position, or judgement—your **conclusion**. When you are writing an argumentative essay, your ultimate goal is to construct an argument that convinces others to *accept your conclusion based upon the premises you've provided.*

Before you can construct an argument for or against someone else's position, you have to appreciate what that person is talking about. You would not be well thought of if you interrupted someone and said, "Hey Buddy, I have no idea what you're talking about, but I think you're wrong!" Unfortunately, as ridiculous as this sounds, this sort of thing happens regularly. Some people will reject an argument simply because they don't like its conclusion, without ever trying to understand the underlying reasoning. To be a good critical thinker, you must do your best to understand other people's claims and arguments.

Once you understand what is being argued, you need to identify each premise and the conclusion and see how they work together. *Only after you understand the entire argument can you go on to evaluate it and respond to it.* Obviously, you have to know what the other person is trying to claim—and what reasons they are giving in support of that claim—before you can determine whether they are right or not. Accordingly, you need to learn about the structure of arguments, how to standardize them, how to determine if the premises are satisfactory, and how to figure out whether they offer sufficient support for the conclusion. The guidelines presented here will be applicable to all sorts of arguments that you will encounter and construct.

Although arguing with another person usually involves some level of disagreement, this is not necessarily a negative thing; it can give you a chance to learn from each other or to work together to find some common ground. For example, you might appear to disagree about a particular topic only because you are using the same words but meaning something different by them. For instance, if you are

Argument: A set of statements in which some statements (premises) are used to support another statement (the conclusion).

Premise: A reason that is used in an argument to support a conclusion.

Conclusion: The part of an argument that the premises are meant to demonstrate by means of evidence or justification.

disagreeing with a colleague over whether the rich should pay more taxes, you might in fact just mean different things by the word "rich." Perhaps a rich person to you is someone who makes $100,000 per year, whereas your colleague thinks it refers to someone who makes $500,000.

When arguing with someone, you might agree on the evidence but draw different conclusions from it. You might think the evidence (e.g., the name of the gentleman) points to Mr. Weiss being from Austria, while your colleague thinks the evidence shows that he is from Germany. Once the matter is settled, you might examine who has made the mistake and why. It has been said many times before, but it is true nonetheless, that you can learn from mistakes—be they yours or someone else's.

If all you did was argue and disagree with people, you wouldn't have too many friends. However, since argumentation is an important feature of our intellectual lives, in the following pages you will (1) learn how to recognize arguments from other types of speech, (2) examine a variety of different types of arguments, (3) learn about how language is used in creating these arguments, and (4) learn how to evaluate them. By learning all of this, you will also be learning how to create your own arguments.

So let's get started!

1.3 Critical Thinking and Reasoning

Arguing isn't just about disagreeing. It isn't just a matter of saying "You're wrong!" or "You're right!" *When evaluating someone's argument, you have to provide an argument in return.* You have to provide premises and a conclusion. You have to say, "I disagree with you because ..."; otherwise, you are not offering an argument—and not being very helpful either! After careful reflection and examination, you may discover that the other person isn't wrong, or you may even find that you can help him or her make his or her argument stronger by making suggestions about what to add, remove, or alter. For example, if a child told you that all birds are black, you might point to a blue jay and say, "There's a bird that isn't black, so you shouldn't say 'all birds,' you should say 'some birds.'" In this case, you would be helping the child learn something new about the world rather than merely telling the child that he or she is wrong. That's how simple and useful critical thinking can be!

Since critical thinking involves thinking (which shouldn't be a surprise to you), it's an activity. Let us repeat that: *critical thinking is an activity.* When you read or hear something critically, you cannot be passive; rather, you must be engaged with the words of the author or speaker. You may sometimes find yourself in agreement with a person's conclusion although your reasons aren't the same as theirs. Or you may believe that their conclusion is false and that their reasoning is flawed too. In either case, you'll have to present your own argument to show why you disagree.

Emotions

Rational Persuasion:
The use of an argument to cause another person to believe a conclusion.

Although arguing with other people is about **rational persuasion**, being rational does not mean we must deny that we are human beings with feelings and emotions. But what is important here—in the context of critical thinking—is that you don't let your emotions get in the way of your reasoning. You are not going to convince (that is, persuade) others to feel the same way you do just because you happen to have certain emotions. It doesn't make sense to claim that one person should be happy or sad simply because someone else is. However, when your emotions start to stir, try to determine why you are feeling them. That is, if you are feeling angry or afraid, ask yourself, "Why?" If you are feeling excited or sad, why? By looking inward and examining your own emotions, you may be able to discover their cause and turn them into reasons for your argument.

Perhaps you are angry about a court decision that you heard about on television. What is it that is making you upset? There is the objective reality—the facts of the matter—and then there is your evaluation of those facts. In this case, your view might be that the judge made a bad ruling and the convicted criminal is not being punished enough or at all for a horrendous crime. Fine. But what exactly is motivating your assessment that the ruling was bad? Do you believe in "an eye for an eye" and that, therefore, this person is not being treated justly? Do you believe that a person who commits bodily harm deserves more punishment than a person who steals the life savings of the elderly? Do you believe that the criminal in question remains a threat to society? Why? Questions like these can help you to focus your attention on determining why you first had this feeling of anger.

Intuition

Critical thinking is not about intuition. Intuition is that vague feeling that is captured by saying "I have a gut reaction to this" or "my instinct tells me that...." You may be hard-pressed to articulate why you feel the way you do when you attribute a feeling to an "intuition." And if *you* can't articulate the "why," then no one else can evaluate the feeling, and you cannot use it to rationally convince others. That you have a gut reaction or feeling about something does not guarantee that another person will share that feeling with you. Stating, for example, "I felt that there was just something odd about what was going on there" only reveals your own reaction to the situation and not how another person should think about it. Try and analyze your feelings and see if there is something more concrete and specific that you can express or explain.

The failure of intuition to be satisfactory in convincing others is why you should always avoid using the expression "I feel" when what you really mean is "I believe." That is, when you are attempting to rationally persuade someone, never say, "I *feel* this is the right answer." Say, "I *believe* this is the right answer." Your gut feeling may be enough to persuade you of a conclusion, but it is not by itself enough to persuade others. Saying "I feel" doesn't carry the same influential weight as "I believe." Notice also, that sometimes it might even be wiser to not even say, "I believe that this is the right answer" but to instead say, "This *is* the right answer." But you will read more about this later on in the book.

Common Sense

Critical thinking is also not just a matter of appealing to "common sense." Common sense may refer to basic logical principles that tell us, for example, that an object can't be green all over and not green all over at the same time or that a person cannot be in two different places at the same time. But what you think may be just a matter of common sense can be and often is wrong. Common sense tells you that the sun moves around the earth, but you know that's not true. Common sense tells you that you should try to steer out of a skid in your car, when in fact you should steer into it. Common sense tells you to try to swim out of a riptide, but in fact you should swim with it until it dissipates.

What was common sense 100 years ago might not be so today. For example, back then it was "obvious" that women shouldn't have the right to vote. This historical reality suggests that some of what people take as common sense now may be seen as superstitious or ignorant in the future. Indeed, many people believe that you will get stomach cramps and drown if you go swimming right after eating. Wrong. Many believe that you will catch a cold if you are physically cold (no, colds are a virus) or that stress is the most common cause of ulcers (no; and although this was a very commonly held view—even by medical science—ulcers were discovered a few years ago to be most often caused by the bacterium *Helicobacter pylori*). These commonsense views are all false, as are the following widespread medical myths:

Finger nails and hair grow after death. This is false; the soft skin around the nails and hair shrinks after death, giving the illusion of nail and hair growth.

Shaved hair grows back faster, coarser, and darker. This is false; the characteristics of newly grown hair change over time, regardless of whether the hair has been shaved.

People only use 10 per cent of their brains. This is false; MRI scans show that no part of our brain is ever inactive.

Reading in dim light causes permanent eye damage. This is false; though reading in dim light might cause some temporary eye strain, after rest the eyes will be back to normal.

Eating turkey makes one especially drowsy. This is false; there is no greater amount of tryptophan (the "sleep chemical") in turkey than in other meats (the drowsiness that many experience after a hearty Thanksgiving meal is the result of a number of factors, not turkey-eating itself).

What an individual considers common sense may depend upon a number of factors including age, gender, culture, social norms, religion, educational background, personal bias, tradition, perception, scientific claims, and so forth. The claim that is being made here is not that your common sense is always wrong; rather, that what may be common sense to you may not be for the person next to you. If you think something is just "common sense," then it should be easy to show it by means of a successful argument.

Arguments vs. Unsupported Claims

Unsupported Claim:
A statement offered without any supporting evidence or argument.

When you say, "I like the current mayor's views," "It's probably going to rain tomorrow," or "The Leafs are going to win the Cup this year!" without offering any reasons for what you've said, you are providing only an **unsupported claim**. An unsupported claim is a statement that is offered without any supporting argumentation or evidence. Unsupported claims are extremely common, and they can be useful, since in many contexts it's entirely reasonable to accept a claim without requiring an argument. Suppose you're at a restaurant and your server tells you that the steak is on special; it would be rather ridiculous to demand further evidence before believing the server's claim! Unsupported claims can also tell us about what a person likes and believes. If you claim that "Chocolate ice cream is the best," there's no need for me to ask for further support; you've told me something about yourself that doesn't require any evidence.

Unsupported claims can be harmless, as in "I thought the movie was great!," but they can also be perilous. Imagine that someone offers the claim that "Capital punishment is wrong" without any support. Also imagine that you happen to agree with this declaration. You might therefore conclude that this person is extremely wise and someone with whom you should become friends. However, although you both have the same belief, the reasons behind the belief may be vastly different. You may believe that capital punishment is wrong because (you believe) it is cruel and unusual punishment (and notice you've provided an argument now, so your claim is no longer unsupported). Yet, if pressed to make an argument, your new best friend might say that capital punishment is wrong because it is too good for the criminal! In its place, your friend might believe that criminals should be strung up and tortured for the rest of their natural lives and that when they are about to die from old age, their lives should be prolonged for even more cruelty. Your new friend might believe that since violent criminals aren't concerned over how much suffering they cause their victims, we shouldn't execute them painlessly. "Capital punishment is wrong because it is too merciful!" Not quite what you assumed your new best friend thought, is it?

The lesson to be learned about unsupported claims is simple. If someone makes an unsupported claim about an important topic, such as capital punishment, you should ask, "Why do you think that?" In other words, *try to turn an unsupported claim into a conclusion of an argument by asking "Why?."* "Why is capital punishment wrong (or right)?" "Why do you think that actor is the best?" "Why is that candidate not suitable to hold public office?" Only after the person has supplied you with his or her justification will you have something to evaluate. The person's premises might not be the best—in fact, they might be downright absurd—but at least now you have an argument that you can work with. And as such, you can begin to assess whether you should agree or disagree based upon the reasons provided. Any reason, no matter how silly, is more useful than no reason.

1.4 Premises and Conclusions: The Building Blocks of Arguments

Arguments have two parts. One part is the point of view, evaluation, judgement, or belief that the argument is attempting to demonstrate. This is the conclusion. The conclusion requires reasons, evidence, foundations, or supporting claims; these make up the other part of the argument and are known as premises. The premises and the conclusion are complete statements that are either true or false. Not sentences: **statements**. Statements are also referred to as "propositions." For example:

Statement: The expression of a single idea or concept; can be either true or false. Also known as a "proposition" or a "claim."

> It's cloudy outside and it's cold, but the forecast for tomorrow calls for clear skies.

This is one sentence with more than one statement. It has three statements: (1) It's cloudy outside. (2) It's cold. (3) The forecast for tomorrow calls for clear skies. All of these are individually capable of being true or false.

Here's another sentence that has two distinct statements in it:

> Dogs can make good pets and cats can make good pets.

The word "and" is joining the statements "dogs can make good pets" and "cats can make good pets" together.

Let's build up an argument. Here's a distinct complete statement:

> Dogs can make good pets.

Here's another:

> Cats can make good pets.

Both of these statements can be true; that is, "Dogs can make good pets" can be true and so can "Cats can make good pets." Of course, both of these can be false as well. Further information may be required to determine if either one is true. You will read about this in Chapter 6. Let's add a bit more detail:

> Dogs can make good pets and cats can make good pets. John and Jane would like to have a good pet. Therefore, John and Jane should consider getting a dog or a cat.

This is not the world's most exciting argument, but it will do. The argument has three premises that logically flow to the conclusion. (1) Dogs can make good pets and (2) cats can make good pets. (3) John and Jane would like to have a good pet. Therefore, John and Jane should consider getting a dog or a cat.

One thing you might notice is the word "therefore." This word is commonly used to indicate the conclusion of an argument. In formal logic, this word has its own symbol: ∴

Indicator Words

Conclusion Indicator:
A word or phrase that signals that a conclusion is being offered.

Premise Indicator:
A word or phrase that signals that there is a premise being offered.

There are many **conclusion indicator** words and many **premise indicator** words. Use these the way you would use route markers on a map; they provide direction and will guide you through arguments. Indicator words help your colleagues follow the flow of your argument and so are extremely useful. Look for them in other people's arguments and include them in your own.

> *Since* the economy has yet to improve *because* no one is spending money, *I conclude* that it would not be wise to take out a large student loan.

This long sentence forms an argument because it has premises and a conclusion. The premise indicators "since" and "because" and the conclusion indicator "I conclude" make the argument's reasoning obvious. Be careful though because a few indicator terms have other meanings as well. For example, "I've been here since 8 a.m." uses "since" as a measurement of time passing.

You already use, or are familiar with, many indicator words, even if you didn't know what they were technically called. Here's a list of a few common ones. (Note: the terms "premise" and "conclusion" and "P" and "C" would be replaced with the appropriate statements.)

> **\<Premise Indicator> Premise**
> \<Since> P
> \<Because> P
> \<For the reason that> P
> \<Given that> P
>
> **\<Conclusion Indicator> Conclusion**
> \<So> C
> \<Thus> C
> \<Hence> C
> \<It follows that> C
> \<Consequently> C
> \<Therefore> C

Premise <Conclusion Indicator> Conclusion

P <shows that> C

P <leads us to believe that> C

P <suggests that> C

Conclusion <Premise Indicator> Premise

C <was proven by> P

C <was established by> P

C <follows from> P

You also use other phrases such as "I think that" or "in my view" to indicate premises and conclusions. If there are no indicator words in the passage that you are examining, it is often useful to insert them yourself to see if an argument "pops out." This is a handy trick when you know that you are dealing with an argument but are not sure of its exact logical structure (i.e., you are not sure if a particular statement is a premise or a conclusion). Here is an example where the conclusion is obvious even though there are no indicator words present:

> Television networks are changing over to high definition digital transmissions. You should get a digital receiver or a new television soon.

If you were not certain that the second sentence is the conclusion, you might put in an indicator word such as "because" or "therefore" or "since" and see what makes common, grammatical, and logical sense. Which of the following sounds better to you?

   1. Since television networks are changing over to high definition digital transmissions, you should get a digital receiver or a new television soon.

or

   2. Television networks are changing over to high definition digital transmissions, since you should get a digital receiver or a new television soon.

Surely the first version represents the correct logical progression. Indeed, it just sounds better too.

As stated at the beginning of this chapter, you already possess critical thinking abilities. Another ability you already have is the ability to recognize how words provide information about the sequence of a group of statements. Consider:

> Afterwards, I ordered a cheesecake. I had a delicious gourmet hamburger at that new pub the other night.

This sounds a bit awkward, doesn't it? If you just stopped after the first sentence, your colleagues would likely be confused. They might ask, "After what?" However, because you know this feature of proper sentence construction, you might automatically reverse the sentences so that people can follow your train of thought:

> I had a delicious gourmet hamburger at that new pub the other night. Afterwards, I ordered a cheesecake.

This next example shows you how simple words help establish the flow of events:

> He woke up. He then had a shower. Finally, he got dressed before heading off to work for the remainder of the day.

Here, you know the first thing happened, then the next thing, and then the next, because the words create a timeline. The word "then" indicates that something happened before, namely, that the person woke up before stepping into the shower (and it makes sense that it would happen in this order!). In the last sentence, the words "finally" and "before" make the ordering of events explicit. Moreover, because this ordering of events is not unusual, we accept it as stated. That is, if the sentence was "He headed off to work for the remainder of the day before he got dressed," you would pause and most likely read the sentence again to see if you read it incorrectly or the author had made a mistake.

Here's a longer example for you to play with. The following sentences are scrambled. Rearrange them so that the passage makes sense.

1. He then added three provinces to the country.
2. As the driving force behind Confederation, John A. Macdonald was appointed the new country's first prime minister, subsequently winning the election.
3. Such fundamental contributions deserve our recognition.
4. Certainly, if we Canadians can have a statutory holiday for Queen Victoria, we can have a special day for the Father of Confederation.
5. These were as follows: Manitoba became a part of Canada in 1870, followed by British Columbia in 1871 and Prince Edward Island in 1873.
6. Later, after the formation of the Dominion of Canada on July 1, 1867, he was knighted.

The correct order is 2, 6, 1, 5, 3, and 4:

2. As the driving force behind Confederation, John A. Macdonald was appointed the new country's first prime minister, subsequently winning the election.
6. Later, after the formation of the Dominion of Canada on July 1, 1867, he was knighted.
1. He then added three provinces to the country.
5. These were as follows: Manitoba became a part of Canada in 1870, followed by British Columbia in 1871 and Prince Edward Island in 1873.
3. Such fundamental contributions deserve our recognition.
4. Certainly, if we Canadians can have a statutory holiday for Queen Victoria, we can have a special day for the Father of Confederation.

While you might not be directly aware of how you figured it out just by looking at it, ordering these sentences required you to see the connections between various terms (such as the sequence of several dates) and how some words reference others or have particular meanings that only make sense when they are in a certain order. This is another example of you being a critical thinker. Proper order is important in argumentation so that people understand your reasoning process.

Making Arguments User Friendly

As you may have noticed, *the conclusion and premises can be located anywhere within a written or spoken argument.* The first statement might be a conclusion and the last statement might be a premise. The conclusion might have a premise before it and one after it. This can happen, for example, when you tack on another reason at the end, as in the following argument:

> Physiotherapy is very useful in speeding up the healing process. This is why physiotherapy should be covered by health care rather than people having to pay for it out of their own pockets. Oh, and in addition, it is actually cheaper both in the short term and long term to have more people go to physiotherapists than for them to wait until they need expensive surgery.

Not everything that is present in an argumentative passage or essay is necessarily a core part of the argument. If all you had in your paragraphs was premise, premise, conclusion, it would be very monotonous. By adding background comments, personal asides, introductory remarks, or even a joke or two, you can make the paragraph more interesting. Of course, how appropriate this is depends upon who your intended audience is and whether you are putting together an informal talk or formal essay. Extra information has been added to the argument below, to fill it out:

> I really enjoy travelling. I've been many places so I can offer a few bits of advice. I had to learn some of these the hard way! If you are planning on visiting Europe this summer, it is a good idea to learn a few basic foreign words and expressions because there are so many opportunities to travel, and if you are lost, you increase your chances of getting help by being able to communicate with the people there. By the way, I found the people in Eastern Europe to be the most helpful.

The extra bits of detail just make it more readable. Nevertheless, it should be clear that the person is trying to convince you that you should learn a few foreign words if you are travelling to Europe.

If you're unsure whether or not a person is making an argument, ask yourself whether he or she is trying to convince you of anything. The way to determine this is to look for the main point. Ask yourself, "Okay, what is going on here? *What is the main point or idea here?*" Every argument has to have one. Once you find the main idea, you've very likely found the conclusion of the argument!

1.5 Identifying Statements and Arguments

Things such as questions ("How are you today?"), jokes ("A man walks into a bar. He should have ducked."), commands ("Close the door."), and emotive expressions ("Ouch!") all have an important role to play in human communication, but they are not means to rationally persuade others. The goal of an arguer is to convince you of something. He or she wants to prove something to you. One way to make you accept his or her view is to threaten you with physical violence if you don't. While this might be an effective method (that is, you don't want to disagree with someone who is telling you he or she will pop you in the jaw if you don't see eye to eye with him or her), it's not good arguing. Indeed, a threat of violence is but one example of bad arguing that you will see later on in Chapter 6, concerning fallacies—but right now it is important to make sure that you can become an expert at playing "spot the argument!" No prizes will be awarded; however, with practice, you will become a little quicker in picking out arguments from non-arguments.

Read the following lighthearted passages and try to determine if any of them are arguments. (More serious ones will be presented later.) If you don't think it is an argument, then try to determine what it is.

1. Because my dog doesn't talk to me, and given that my vegetables don't talk to me, it follows that my dog is a vegetable.
2. It has been very dry and hot for the past few months, and there is a strong breeze coming from over the forest hills. There is also a smoky smell in the air. Therefore, Gouda cheese is good for you.
3. The leaders of the Western world sat down together for a big bowl of ice cream.
4. If everyone in the southern hemisphere jumped up and down right now, then the earth would move to the right.
5. Would you kindly remove your boot from my backside?
6. The universe does not revolve around you, it revolves around me!
7. The universe is big.
8. Put your clothes back on please.
9. Mmmmm!
10. Bunny rabbits and beer go well together, since both are full of hops.
11. It is true that it is either a Blix or a Phregerel. It is also true that it cannot be a Blix. So it must be a Phregerel.
12. "Arghei blh!" is the first sentence of the author's latest novel—225 pages of randomly selected letters from the keyboard. The book costs $18.95.
13. It is a very stupid idea for a book. If I were to review it, I would say it is a bunch of !@#%$.
14. It took a while, but the coroner was able to determine that the cause of the man's death was that he stopped breathing for a very, very long time—most likely due to the fact that his head was missing.
15. Why don't people use fake money to pay for plastic surgery?

You are not going to be told just yet what the answers are. However, here is a hint. There are four arguments above. Go back and check.

Did you find four?

Good.

Wait.

Did you pick the right four?

You will find out momentarily, but first you need to learn a bit more about the differences between arguments and non-arguments. It is only when you have identified that you are dealing with an argument that you can then proceed to analyze its various components and evaluate whether you should accept it or reject it. If it is not an argument, although the sentence or passage may still be quite interesting and useful, it is not an example of rational persuasion.

Non-Statements

As mentioned earlier, not all sentences are statements. Some sentences contain multiple statements, while other sentences contain no statements at all. Remember that a statement makes a claim that is either true or false. In this section, we'll examine some common types of sentences that may look like statements but in fact are not. Since statements are the building blocks of arguments, we need to be able to identify statements in order to identify arguments.

QUESTIONS AND RHETORICAL QUESTIONS

Questions are not meant to be true or false claims intended to convince one of anything. To say a question is true or false is to say something odd indeed. "Will you take the garbage out today?" is just a question, not a "true" question. If you replied that you will take the garbage out and do in fact take it out, then that statement (that is, "I will take the garbage out") is what is true.

Sometimes people phrase statements as if they were questions. These are known as **rhetorical questions**. *A rhetorical question is used when the person believes that the answer is already known and it is perceived as being obvious.* So, really, the person isn't waiting for your response at all. Rhetorical questions such as "It really doesn't matter if I come to class today, does it?," "What good is having a law if you cannot enforce it?," "Why should I care about others if they don't care about me?," and "You really don't want me to answer that, do you?" should all be treated as statements that can be true or false. They should be rewritten so that their meaning is clear: "It doesn't matter if I come to class today." "Laws that cannot be enforced are not good laws." "People don't care about me, and I am not going to care about them." "You won't like the answer if I respond to your question."

Rhetorical questions are problematic because they can, and often do, backfire. They often take the form "Everyone knows that *such and such* is true, right?" To claim that everyone knows something is a pretty strong statement to make and

Rhetorical Question: A question that has an implied answer and therefore functions as a statement.

also an easy one to refute since you only need to find one person who doesn't know that such and such is true (perhaps even you!). Usually, people who try to claim that "everyone knows" do so as a strategic manoeuvre to intimidate the listener into thinking that somehow he or she is in the wrong (and is stupid as well) because so many people know "better."

COMMANDS

Commands are not statements because they are not capable of being true or false. Commands telling someone to take out the garbage or to make sure that his or her shoes are tied are authoritative requests, not statements of fact. Rules and laws are also examples of commands, but one has to be careful. If the command is "Do the dishes," it is neither true nor false. But if the command is "You *should* do the dishes," then this is not a command but something that is debatable—it is a statement you can argue over (namely, whether or not it is true that you should do the dishes).

Although the command "Do not park your car here" is neither a true claim nor a false one, you can still debate whether someone has good reason to obey it. For example, is the law arbitrary? Is the law discriminatory? Is there a large fine for disobeying? These all provide (good or bad) reasons for drawing a particular conclusion, and so they will be true or false—but the original command itself is neither true nor false.

EMOTIVE EXPRESSIONS

Ouch! Ugh! Wha??? Argh! Whew! Grrr! Brrr! Bah! Blah! Ow!

When people utter these sorts of expressions, you can understand and appreciate their sentiments. They are vocalizing some feeling or state of being that is positive or negative. But consider this: if someone said, "Ouch!" to you, would you agree or disagree with him or her? Would you say, "I don't think so. I think you are mistaken"? Of course you wouldn't. You don't evaluate these sorts of communications as being correct or incorrect or true or false. Merely expressing one's own emotions is not an attempt to argue. If a person is whimpering in pain, she is not saying anything right or wrong. She is just expressing how she feels.

Now, looking back over the 15 examples above, are any of them just vocalizations of someone's emotional state?

Found it? Right. It's number 9. Yeah!! Woo-hoo!!!!

Okay, that's enough cheerleading emotive expressing for now. ☺

(And perhaps you notice the smiley face at the end of that sentence. It also represents an emotive expression.)

Thankfully, not everything that comes out of your mouth involves trying to make a point or convince someone of something. When you slam your hand in the car door, a passerby is not going to disagree with the words that come out of your mouth. He or she might help you, feel sorry for you, laugh at you, or tell you not to use such foul language in public, but the noise that escaped your lips was not an argument. Indeed, unlike when you wish to construct an argument, these sorts of expressions are often immediate and are vocalized without any prior thought.

Be careful. You don't want to confuse these emotive examples with similar sounding expressions such as "Super!" "Dazzling!" "Fantastic!" "Awesome!" "Magnificent!" "Boring!" "Horrible!" "Electrifying!" Although these particular terms express a person's attitude towards something (or some event or person or what-have-you), and although it would seem odd to think that "super!" is true or false, in fact in certain contexts saying "super" is a shorthanded way of saying "I believe that thing (or event or person or what-have-you) is wonderful." You may actually agree or disagree with the view that the person is conveying with the term, but, again, you will need to make further inquiries.

Non-Arguments

Not every passage that contains statements is an argument. Even if a passage contains nothing but statements, it may not be an attempt to support a conclusion on the basis of premises. In this section, we'll examine descriptions and explanations, which are easily mistaken for arguments if you're not looking carefully.

DESCRIPTIONS

Descriptions of events are not arguments. *Descriptions are declarations concerning how the world was, is, or will be*; they can be either true or false. "Sarah graduated from university in June 2012." "Today was eight degrees warmer than the average temperature and the sun was shining." "The truck is available in four colours: black, red, blue, or white." Merely describing something is not arguing, because it does not involve using premises to support a conclusion. Of course, descriptions can be part of an argument, such as when a person complains:

Description: A statement or set of statements concerning how the world was, is, or will be.

> The movie *Meet my Pets* was 84 minutes long including the credits (description). Most people would complain about such a short film (unsupported claim). However, when a comedy film is not funny at all it seems to make time slow down to a crawl (unsupported claim). So, *Meet my Pets* was too long—by about an hour (conclusion).

Here, the description of the movie's length is a statement that is used as a premise in an argument, though the description is not an argument on its own.

EXPLANATIONS

When people offer **explanations** as to why the sun rises (or, to be more correct, why it appears to us that the sun rises), or how a computer program works, or how planes are able to stay aloft, or how someone contracts an illness, they are trying to show why something is the way it is. We experience many things in the world, and, due to our capacity for curiosity and wonder, we want to understand how those things

Explanation: An attempt to show why some fact is true by appealing to contributing factors.

come about. "Why can I see stars that are billions of kilometres away yet have to wear glasses to read street signs?" "Why do dogs sometimes wag their tails when they are sleeping?" "Why do people in horror movies always run back into the darkened house where the killer is?" In answering questions such as these—questions about why things are the way they are—an explanation identifies **factors**, or causes.

Factor: A fact or event that causes or influences another fact or event.

Suppose that you and I are on the same stationary train and are having the same experience of non-motion. The fact is that the train is not moving. I don't have to prove this to you. But what is the cause? What are the factors behind the fact? Perhaps there is an obstruction ahead.

Consider the fact that a person is dead. I don't have to kick him a few times to prove to you that he is dead. We both see that his head is located three metres away from his body. What we want to determine is what led to his death. Maybe it was an accident, maybe it was murder. What clues do we have to help us establish the fact that this person's death was intentional? We are not arguing that he is dead; rather, we are trying to explain the cause of his death. We want to figure out what the factors are that led to the fact that we are witnessing.

The logical progression of a causal explanation is always from the observation or the fact to the causal factors that explain it. This is the exact opposite of an argument, where the arguer moves from the reasons to the conclusion. There may be a "conclusion" that there is a stopped train or a dead body, but those are the givens; we want to find out how they came about—and that is why it is an explanation and not an argument. Or consider when the instructor says to the student, "Why are you late?" and the student replies, "Because I couldn't find a parking spot." Here the student's answer is an explanation. She is providing the causal factor. Both the student and the instructor can see by the clock on the wall that she is late.

Of course, *not all explanations are scientific or causal in nature.* Another use of an explanation might be when someone is confused, say, about the meaning of a word. In Chapter 2 you'll learn about different types of definitions, but simply put, if a person doesn't understand a word, you would offer an explanation of it. You wouldn't provide an argument to try to convince him or her of its proper meaning. You might explain the word by simply giving an example of what it refers to. Imagine you are asked, "What is a hound?" and you say, "It's a type of dog that was historically used in hunting." But perhaps this is not clear, and so you might offer another example by mentioning a specific breed such as a beagle or whippet. In doing so, you are explaining the concept "hound." You are not arguing that such and such should be considered a "hound."

Recognizing Arguments and Other Expressions

Let's go through the light-hearted questions from earlier in the chapter and see what sorts of expressions they are.

1. Because my dog doesn't talk to me and given that my vegetables don't talk to me, it follows that my dog is a vegetable.

This is an argument. There are two premises (1) My dog doesn't talk to me. (2) My vegetables don't talk to me. There are two premise indicators ("because" and "given that"). The two premises are being used to try and establish the (very silly) conclusion that the person's dog is a vegetable. This example shows the use of indicators.

2. It has been very dry and hot for the past few months, and there is a strong breeze coming from over the forest hills. There is also a smoky smell in the air. Therefore, Gouda cheese is good for you.

This is an argument. The first two sentences are the premises and the conclusion is identified with the use of the indicator word "therefore." One might have expected that the person was developing an argument that perhaps there is a forest fire, given the premises mentioned, but that is not the case; the conclusion has nothing to do with the premises. This example shows that even bad arguments are still arguments.

3. The leaders of the Western world sat down together for a big bowl of ice cream.

This is a just a silly description.

4. If everyone in the southern hemisphere jumped up and down right now, then the earth would move to the right.

No evidence is offered to convince you of its truth, so in this context it is an unsupported claim.

5. Would you be upset if I asked you to kindly remove your boot from my backside?

This is an example of a question.

6. The universe does not revolve around you, it revolves around me!

This sentence contains two statements, neither of which is supported. We might, however, interpret this as an argument if we rephrase it as follows: "The universe revolves around me, so it does not revolve around you." Note also that the use of an exclamation mark does not make the claim any more effective. Saying something loud or more than once doesn't make it any truer.

7. The universe is big.

This is an unsupported claim. Furthermore, the term "big" is pretty vague and open to subjective interpretation. How big is big?

8. Put your clothes back on please.

This is a command. It is telling you to do something. It is neither a true nor a false statement.

9. Mmmmm!!

This is an emotive expression. The person is merely vocalizing his or her pleasure and is not trying to convince you of anything. The person would be trying to convince you if he or she went on to state "Because it is yummy, you should try it too."

10. Bunny rabbits and beer go well together, since both are full of hops.

This is an argument. The conclusion that "bunny rabbits and beer go well together" is based upon the premise that bunny rabbits and beer have something in common (i.e., one contains "hops" as an ingredient and one "hops" around). The word "since" is a premise indicator.

11. It is true that it is either a Blix or a Phregerel. It is also true that it cannot be a Blix. So it must be a Phregerel.

This is an argument. The conclusion indicator word is "so." The point of this example is that you do not need to know what the subject matter of an argument is in order to see its logical structure. The structure of this particular argument goes like this: A or B. Not B. So A.

12. "Arghei blh!" is the first sentence of the author's latest novel—225 pages of randomly selected letters from the keyboard. The book costs $18.95.

This is a description of a very strange book.

13. It is a very stupid idea for a book. If I were to review it, I would say it is a bunch of #$$@vq!!

This is a group of statements. Notice that the person does not give evidence for the claim that the idea for the book is stupid, so that claim is unsupported.

14. It took a while, but the coroner was able to determine that the cause of the man's death was that he stopped breathing for a very, very long time. This was most likely due to the fact that his head was missing.

This is an explanation. You don't need to prove that the man is dead. Rather, you need to determine the cause of his death. And you should probably give the coroner an award for stating the obvious.

15. Why don't people just use fake money to pay for plastic surgery?

This is a rhetorical question. The person is facetiously suggesting that people should use fake money for plastic surgery.

1.6 Chapter Exercises

Exercise 1.1

TRUE/FALSE QUESTIONS

1. This sentence contains an argument. True or False?
2. Premises are supposed to supply support for a conclusion. True or False?
3. When someone gives an argument (in the philosophical sense), he or she maintains that because the argument's premises hold, its conclusion should be granted. True or False?
4. If the premises are satisfactory and if the conclusion is true, then the argument must be good too. True or False?
5. In the argument "The library is a useful place because you can find lots of information there," the statement "You can find lots of information there" is the premise. True or False?

Exercise 1.2

Can you identify which of the following passages are arguments? If you find an argument, what are the premises and the conclusion? Are there any indicator words?

1. After being told that I did not have the authority to order more stock, I was starting to get a little worked up. I paused a moment and then looked my boss straight in the eye. "Sir, I cannot believe that you didn't know I was being left in charge of the entire store while you were on vacation in Hawaii."
2. If you want to make your canned drinks cold fast, put them in a bowl of ice water and add a handful of salt. The salt will lower the freezing temperature of the water and will cause your drinks to cool down rapidly.
3. I have a patio deck that needs replacing. It is about three metres by six. The original wood was not sealed properly by the previous owners. The wood is rotting away, so it needs to be taken off and replaced. The same goes for the wooden railing too.
4. The spark that started World War I was the assassination by Serbian nationalists of Archduke Franz Ferdinand, heir to the Austro-Hungarian throne, in Sarajevo on June 28, 1914. Austria issued an ultimatum to the Serbian government to participate in the conviction of the assassins. When this demand was rejected, Austria went to war. Russia had a treaty to help Serbia and joined in the fight. Germany, on the other hand, had an agreement with Austria and declared war on Russia. France joined with Russia, and then Britain allied with France and declared war on Germany.

5. The Canadian city of Winnipeg, which has a population of over 500,000 people, has the honour of being the coldest city on Earth. In the winter (which seems to last for most of the year), it regularly goes to -40 degrees. Growing up, I remember walking to school in the bitter cold. The moisture from my eyes would form tiny icicles on my eyelashes. The coldest days were also the sunniest, however. Only when there was a blizzard would classes be cancelled.

6. The lawyers pick jury members on account of their ability to be fair. I told them that I could not honestly say how I might respond if I was put in a situation where I might have to sacrifice the life of a loved one, and I think that this is good enough to conclude that I would be fair. Accordingly, I expect to be chosen for the jury.

7. There seem to be vast climate changes affecting the planet. There are hotter summers in one place, colder winters in another, and wetter springs in others. These events tell us that to just use the term "global warming" is wrong.

8. In the world of professional sports, there is a lot of money at stake. Athletes will try anything, including cheating, to win. Coming in second is not an option for some athletes who know that winning means fame and fortune.

9. If you are planning on visiting Europe this summer, it is a good idea to learn a few basic foreign words and expressions because there are so many opportunities to travel, and if you are lost, you increase your chances of getting help by being able to communicate.

Exercise 1.3

In your local newspaper, find a short letter to the editor that you believe contains an argument. Make a copy of the original and then cut the sentences out and give them to a colleague after you randomly sort them. Can your colleague put them back in the original order?

Exercise 1.4

Imagine you are in the advertising business. Create a print ad for a new product (e.g., a car, a soft drink, a movie, a vacation spot) using an example of five different types of communication from those discussed above. For instance:

Do you want a new car? (question) Buy this one (command). It is very stylish (unsupported claim). It is available in a two-door and a four-door model (description). You surely don't want to be seen driving something less impressive than this, do you? (rhetorical question).

Exercise 1.5

What is the main point in the following passages?

1. Let me tell you why I will not take that professor's philosophy course this year. First, it's too hard for me. I've seen the textbook and have no idea what it is about, even after reading the introduction. The class is early in the morning, and you know how I have a hard time waking up. So I'll miss some classes for sure. I'll be stressed out about whether I would pass or fail and that will just make matters worse.
   a. Whether I ought to take the philosophy course.
   b. Whether I will take the philosophy course.
   c. Whether I will be obsessed by the philosophy course.
   d. Whether I find philosophy too difficult.

2. It will take decades to recover from pollution caused by the BP oil leak off the coast of the United States in 2010. Offshore drilling must be stopped. Everything will be affected. Jobs will be lost, tourists will stop visiting, and some wildlife will be wiped out for good. This is all the result of the never-ending consumer desire for more and more oil.
   a. Whether offshore oil drilling must be stopped.
   b. Whether the BP oil leak was indirectly caused by consumer demand.
   c. Whether the US coast line will take decades to recover.
   d. Whether the US economy will take decades to recover.

3. This year's National Hockey League draft lists a large number of goalies available. Many NHL teams need good goalies this year. If you have a lousy goalie, then you are sure not going to win many games! I bet a lot of goalies will be drafted early on.
   a. Whether there are teams in the NHL that need goalies.
   b. Whether there are a large number of goalies available in the player draft this year.
   c. Whether a lot of goalies will be chosen early.
   d. Whether a good goalie will help a team win more games.

4. Most people attending or teaching at university are interested in being challenged by new ideas. Some of these ideas are wild and crazy, but others are more significant and can be considered quite radical in terms of being a threat to what is commonly accepted by society. I just wanted to let you know what to expect this year when you go. Some students and professors you will interact with on campus will be radicals.
   a. Whether people are interested in new things.
   b. Whether you'll find radical thinkers at university.
   c. Whether students are interested more in new ideas than professors are.
   d. Whether common views need to be challenged more in university.

5. Television shows set in ancient Greece or medieval Europe can never be good without all the blood and violence. Without blood and violence, these shows will not capture what the times were really like. Sure the violence we are shown is often shocking, but these were very brutal periods of human history. If the actors just said, "Ouch" or fell down and played dead, viewers would laugh and turn the shows off. Sometimes the violence can be way over the top and offensive to some, but given the nature of these shows, if you don't like the overall setting, you won't like the violence, and vice versa.

   a. Whether shows with offensive characteristics can appeal to those who don't like violence.

   b. Whether television shows set in ancient Greece or medieval Europe would be good television series without the inclusion of violence.

   c. Whether television shows set in ancient Greece or medieval Europe would be believable without the inclusion of violence.

   d. Whether television shows will succeed if they contain content that will be offensive to some.

6. State three different premise indicator words or phrases.

7. State three different conclusion indicator words or phrases.

8. Form an argument using two different indicator words or phrases.

9. Form an argument without using any indicator words or phrases.

10. What should you notice about the word "arguement"?

Exercise 1.6

STATEMENT GENERATOR: MORAL ISSUES STATEMENTS

		a	b		c	d
1	It is	Always	Obligatory	for	Adults	to get on a bus without paying if no one is looking.
2		Usually	Right		Children	to keep a promise even if it hurts someone's feelings.
3		Sometimes	Permissible		Community members	to eat meat.
4		Hardly ever	Wrong		Family members	to allow a 17-year-old to have a friend sleep over in the same room.
5		Never	Prohibited		Friends	to read material that others consider offensive.

Randomly select a number between 1 to 5 for each lettered column in the table above. (You may wish to write down numbers on scraps of paper, place them face down and select one at a time, returning the paper you have selected to the pile for the next column and your next selection. In this way, you can draw the same number more than once.) Each number corresponds to a word or phrase to create a statement dealing with some ethical issue. Without any support, this statement is just an opinion. Reflecting upon it, ask yourself, "Why?" Then provide reasons for the claim so that you have now created an argument. In this first use of the statement generator, do not be concerned about how good your reasons are. The important thing right now is to just create arguments.

For example: You draw the numbers 2,2,1,4. This creates the unsupported claim:

> It is usually (from column a) good (b) for adults (c) to allow a 17-year-old to have a friend sleep over in the same room (d).

Now you want to provide possible reasons for this claim. You ask, "Why?"

> Seventeen-year-olds are old enough to make their own decisions. If adults don't allow them some degree of control over their lives, they're likely to become frustrated and resentful. Therefore, it is usually good for adults to allow a 17-year-old to have a friend sleep over in the same room.

You have created an argument!

Now you can do the same to generate statements that might come up in a workplace.

STATEMENT GENERATOR: BUSINESS STATEMENTS

		a	b		c	d
1	It is	Always	Obligatory	for	CEOs	to receive large bonuses.
2		Usually	Right		Bosses	to make a living wage.
3		Sometimes	Permissible		Employees	to make environmental concerns their top priority.
4		Hardly ever	Wrong		Family members	to hire a friend over a stranger.
5		Never	Prohibited		Friends	to reveal corporate secrets.

1.7 Postscript

Each chapter of this book flows from the previous one. So make sure you understand the concepts from Chapter 1 before moving on to Chapter 2 and understand Chapter 2 before moving on to Chapter 3, and so forth.

With this first chapter, you were presented with a few different types of oral and written communication. While many everyday utterances are interesting and helpful, they are not always contextually relevant here. Thus, by themselves, unsupported claims, emotive expressions (which reveal how a person feels), sincere questions (which are neither true nor false as opposed to true or false statements that are dressed up as rhetorical questions), commands, jokes, and explanations are not part of rational persuasion. But being able to identify when they occur is part of critical thinking. You might wish to criticize a person for making a bad joke or an inappropriate comment, but that is best left for another time. In what follows in the remaining chapters, you will be working with passages that are intended to rationally persuade others by means of well-constructed arguments.

CHAPTER 2
The Use and Abuse of Language

In this chapter, we'll discuss the various ways in which words possess meaning and the ways in which imprecision in language can lead to confusion and error. Though you may know what you mean when you speak, your audience may misunderstand you if you're not careful in your choice of words. And even when you use the right words, it's often necessary to define them so as to avoid ambiguity, vagueness, and unintended connotation.

2.1 Meaning, Denotation, and Connotation

Choosing the right words for your argument is important. Don't play fast and loose with your word choice—pay precise attention to the meanings of the words you use, and make sure they match your meaning exactly. Say what you mean to say, nothing more and nothing less; don't exaggerate, but also don't play down what you want to say. Are the children's parents *uncaring* or are they *cruel*? "Uncaring" tells you they are not concerned what happens to their children, while "cruel" suggests that they are actively doing something to hurt them. Is the judge *uninterested* or *disinterested* in the court case? These words may sound alike, but they have different meanings. An uninterested judge is unconcerned and doesn't care, while a disinterested judge is objective and fair.

Do not take your selections lightly. The slightest alteration can make all the difference in the world. Though synonyms are words that mean the same thing,

Denotation: What a word literally refers to.

Connotation: Emotional or conceptual associations that are connected to a word but not part of its literal definition.

Multi-vocal: Term applied to words that have more than one meaning.

different synonyms can give people different impressions—their **denotations** are the same, but their **connotations** are different. "Svelte" and "skinny" may literally mean the same thing, but being called skinny might offend someone in a way that being called svelte would not. This is because "skinniness" is often associated with unhealthiness. Thus, it has a negative connotation, whereas "svelte" has a positive connotation.

Which wording would be more appropriate when a friend is wearing a new perfume or cologne: "What is that scent?" or "What is that smell?" Though the two words mean the same thing, one has a positive connotation, while the other has a negative or neutral connotation. What you say can be perceived quite differently depending on which word you choose.

Another reason why you have to take care with words is that most English words are **multi-vocal**. This means that they *can have more than one meaning*. "Pat" is a person's name, but it is also something you can do, such as pat your friend Pat on the back. A "chair" is a piece of furniture, but "chair" also refers to someone who is in charge of a meeting or a university department. "How many chairs are at the meeting?" Well, do you mean things to sit on or administrators? You can charge a battery, take charge, or charge an expense to your credit card. Legendary stand-up comedian (and informal philosopher) George Carlin built his career in part by showing how we use multi-vocal words in weird ways.

The intended meanings of multi-vocal words, such as "Pat," "chair," "free" (as in having "no cost" or as in "liberty"), and "bat" (as in a "baseball bat" or a "vampire bat") are usually clear in the context of their uses. If I say, "Bautista is up to bat," you know perfectly well what I mean. When it is *not* clear which meaning is intended, this can cause problems.

If you understand a speaker's statement to signify one thing, while in fact the speaker intended something else, you will be *arguing at cross purposes*. That is, you will be using the same words when talking but meaning different things and thus not really arguing!

> Bob: I enjoy comics.
> Brenda: Not me; they're obnoxious, especially Louis CK.
> Bob: No, I mean comic books; you know, Superman, Batman, that kind of thing.
> Brenda: Oh! I thought you meant comedians! I like comics too!

Imagine you and Olivia are arguing about the political leanings of a mutual friend:

> Olivia: I think he is a communist.
> You: Why? Because he likes the colour red?
> Olivia: Be serious. The guy supports national health care programs.
> You: So do most Canadians. That doesn't make him a communist.
> Olivia: He thinks the wealthy get away without paying their fair share, that there should be greater equality between how much the rich make and how much the poor make. That's communism.

You: No, that's socialism. Communists don't believe that there should be any inequality. They believe that the state should own everything and that there shouldn't be any private property. That is quite different from what, say, the New Democratic Party would claim.

Your discussion moved away from a factual dispute about whether a certain person is or is not a communist to a dispute about what the word "communist" means. You and Olivia are having a **verbal dispute** about what makes someone a communist. You are trying to establish the essential characteristics of the term "communist" so that you are not arguing about different things even though you are both using the same word. Once you have settled on the meaning of "communist" (and perhaps even clarified the meaning of "wealthy"), you can return to the factual dispute about your friend.

Verbal Dispute: A disagreement about the meaning of a term.

2.2 Defining Words

When you aren't sure what a word means, what are you going to do? No, you shouldn't just skip over it. You should look it up in a dictionary. **Reportive definitions**, sometimes called *lexical definitions*, are definitions of the type that you find in an ordinary dictionary ("lexical" comes from "lexicon," which is Greek for "book of words"). *Reportive definitions identify or report how a word is generally used.* Although the amount of space available for a definition is sometimes too limited to fully explain a term's meaning, dictionaries aim at giving the essential properties shared by all and only those objects referred to by the term.

Reportive Definition: A dictionary-type definition that attempts to capture how a word is normally used.

Sometimes, when writing papers or in everyday life, you may have to create reportive definitions on your own rather than relying on those in the dictionary. When trying to find the right reportive definition of a word, you need to determine what it is that all of the things designated by that word have in common. Why is *this* thing called a chair but not *that* thing? Why is *this* thing called a car and *that* thing a truck? (By the way, if you want to impress someone, you might want to remember that the word that is being looked up in the dictionary is called the **definiendum** and the words that are being used to define it are the **definiens**.)

Definiendum: In a definition, the word that is being defined.

If you wanted to tell someone what a zombie is, you would give a list of the defining properties that make something a zombie. Being undead distinguishes zombies from most other things but not from everything, since vampires and Frankenstein's monster are also undead. That zombies walk slowly separates them from vampires but still not from Frankenstein's monster. But zombies, unlike Frankenstein's monster, like to eat human brains. So we might define zombies as "slow-moving undead creatures that eat human brains." All zombies, but nothing that isn't a zombie, satisfy this definition. And we can see the practical value of having such a precise definition at hand:

Definiens: The definition of a word.

"Who's at the door?"

"Just some undead person."

"Oh, do I need garlic and a cross?"

"Nah, that won't help with a zombie."

"I see—then I'd better put on my helmet!"

Here's another example. Suppose you want to define the word "table." First, you need to clarify that you are referring to the piece of furniture and not a mathematical table. Once that is done, then you have to provide more details. Just being a piece of furniture doesn't distinguish a table from a chair or a sofa or a bed. That it has four legs doesn't help either because chairs, sofas, and beds all can have four legs too. However, a table is primarily used to put objects on rather than to sit or rest on. And so we might propose the following definition of table: a piece of furniture that is designed for putting objects on.

You have to make sure to capture all and only what is essential to what it is you wish to define.

If you left your definition of table as "a piece of furniture," it would be *too broad*, as it would include things that ought not to be included, such as chairs, sofas, and beds. If you went too far in the opposite direction and said that a "table is a piece of furniture that has four legs and is designed for putting objects on and is round and made of wood," then your definition would be *too narrow*, since this definition excludes tables that are square or rectangular in shape or made of materials other than wood. Sometimes definitions can be both too broad and too narrow at the same time. For instance, a definition of "car" as "a means of transportation that is red in colour" would be too broad since trucks and bicycles and airplanes are also means of transportation, and it would be too narrow because cars come in many different colours besides red.

When you are defining a word you need to be sure that your definition is not too broad or too narrow (or both); otherwise, your audience may misinterpret what you are talking about. Some reportive definitions are **vague** too—that is, their meanings are unclear. If you asked your waiter what a "large salad" is and the waiter responded, "It's a very big salad," this would be unhelpful—just how big is "very big"?

Reportive definitions can also suffer from being **circular**. If you looked up the word "student" and the definition you were given was "someone who studies," would you have a better idea of the meaning of the word? If you didn't know what a politician was and were told that a politician is someone who is involved in politics, would you then understand? Not really. These definitions are circular, as they include a word (i.e., "studies" or "politics") in the definiens that forms part of the definiendum.

A definition is **obscure** when it is difficult to understand. Have you ever tried to learn the meaning of a word by looking up its definition in a science or medical dictionary? Many of the definiens are very complex terms themselves and require

Vagueness: When a word or sentence is so unclear that the listener cannot determine its specific meaning.

Circular Definition: A definition in which a word that is included in the definiens is also part of the definiendum.

Obscure Definition: A vague or difficult to understand definiens.

specialized knowledge. Suppose you looked up the word "lie" and found the following definition: "Lie: an anti-veritical state of affairs." This is an obscure definition. Someone who doesn't know what a lie is surely won't understand what a veritical state of affairs is, let alone an anti-veritical one!

If you were unsure what a person meant by a word, you might ask for a **definition by example**. This would require the person to give you examples of what the word denotes (i.e., what it literally refers to). Thus, if you asked what a "conifer" is, the person might say, "Pine trees, spruce trees, and cedar trees are all types of conifer." However, if you are also unfamiliar with those specific tree types, then this denotative definition would not help you understand "conifer." The person might then provide you with an **ostensive definition**, a *non-verbal definition*, whereby he or she simply points to an example of the object in question and says, "That is a conifer." Providing an ostensive definition can be very quick and easy when referring to common objects (e.g., trees, toys, windows) or actions (e.g., yawning, running, laughing). Still, they will only work if the two of you are both looking at the same object! If you ask me what a car is, I might point at one. However, you might believe that I am pointing at the wheels, or the door, or the specific model, or even the colour! Furthermore, one cannot provide an ostensive definition of important concepts such as love, justice, truth, friendship, and motherhood, because it's impossible to point at these things.

Some words are themselves vague and don't allow for a reportive definition because they are used differently by different people. Consider the word "tall," for example—we can't give a precise reportive definition for "tall" because there may be people (at, say, 5'11") whom I would call tall and whom you would say are not tall. In these cases, it is best to give a **stipulative definition** explaining what you personally mean by the word. If you are debating whether a person is wealthy or not, you might say, "By 'wealthy' I mean 'has assets worth more than a million dollars.'" This kind of definition helps us to avoid arguing at cross purposes, as we can now use an otherwise vague term with a precise meaning in mind. If you just used the vague term "wealthy" without first defining it, you and the person you're speaking to might have different notions of what "wealthy" means. If you agree on the facts about how much wealth the person has, but you disagree about whether they are wealthy, you are actually engaged in a verbal dispute about what "wealthy" means and not a factual dispute. Stipulative definitions are often found in specialized fields of study—especially in academics.

Even if your terms are clearly defined, there are still a lot of pitfalls you can encounter when you are writing your own arguments. The following sections outline a few common writing mistakes that can make your argument difficult to interpret or even, in some cases, offensive to other people.

Definition by Example: A definition that appeals to examples of the definiendum in order to illustrate its denotation.

Ostensive Definition: A definition of a word given by a non-verbal action (as when you define the word "jump" by jumping) or by bringing someone's attention to the object the word refers to (as in pointing to a cat to define the word "cat").

Stipulative Definition: A definition whereby the speaker specifies how he or she is using a word, regardless of whether this conforms to normal use.

2.3 Vagueness and Ambiguity

We've already mentioned vagueness—or lack of clarity—as a problem that comes up in definitions, but vagueness can occur anywhere in written or spoken communication. If you asked Jim what a particular movie was about and whether it was worth seeing and he said, "It's about these people who do some cool stuff and then some other neat stuff!," he would be giving you a very vague description. What is the "stuff" that he's referring to? Who are the "people" doing this stuff? And what exactly do "cool" and "neat" mean? Would Jim's description be sufficient for you to decide if you should go see the movie? Certainly not. Vagueness can be problematic in arguments because if people don't have a clear understanding of what you're saying, they won't be able to agree or disagree with you. Here are a few simple examples of vague statements:

> The movie was okay. (What does "okay" mean? Good? Worth watching?)
>
> My vacation was interesting. (Is "interesting" good? Was the vacation enjoyable or not?)
>
> She's nice. (What does "nice" mean? Pleasant? Friendly?)

Although it might be vague to use terms such as "a bit" or "a lot," it isn't always inappropriate to do so. There is nothing wrong with saying "Just add a bit of salt to the recipe." Or if someone asks you, "How much does it hurt?" replying "A bit" or "A lot" is actually more helpful than saying "Exactly three times more than a toothache." And telling someone that you are doing "well" might not be very specific, but it may be inappropriate to go into further detail with a stranger.

Context matters here. If a stranger asked you, "How much money do you make?," would you be specific or vague in your response? On the other hand, if potential employers told you that the salary they would pay you was "a good amount," would you take the job?

Ambiguity occurs when the *words being used have more than one meaning and it is not known which meaning is intended.* Ambiguity is different from vagueness because each of the possible meanings is clear; the part that is unclear is which of the possible meanings is the right one. Here are some examples of ambiguous words and statements:

Ambiguity: When a word or sentence has more than one possible meaning.

> James: She is my partner.
> Jane: Do you mean your work partner or your girlfriend?
>
> TV sports reporter: Are you going to get a goal today?
> Soccer player: I always have a goal. My goal has always been to get a goal.
>
> Fisherman 1: The salmon are being caught by fishers while swimming in the Adams River.
> Fisherman 2: Why are the fishers swimming in the river?!

When a statement is ambiguous, you should ask, "Do you mean X or do you mean Y?" Accordingly, you should not agree or disagree with an ambiguous claim until you know for certain whether the person means X or Y. Consider:

> James: That is Sarah with her mother Silvia over there. She's nice.
> Jane: Do you mean Sarah is nice or do you mean Silvia is nice?

Sometimes the proper interpretation of an ambiguous term is obvious in its context. If someone said, "The clock tells me it is time to go," he or she meant it figuratively and would not be amused if you made some remark such as "Oh, you are listening to and taking orders from clocks, are you?"

Don't confuse vagueness with ambiguity. Remember, if something is vague, it has no precise meaning. If something is ambiguous, it has two or more precise meanings, but it's not obvious which one is intended.

> Vague: Student to professor: I had to spend a great deal of time doing
>   the homework.
> The professor wonders: How much time is that?
>
> Ambiguous: Student to professor: How much longer is this class?
> The professor wonders: Does the student mean "how much longer will the class be
>   today?" or "how many more weeks until the end of semester?"

Ambiguity is a serious problem in arguments because it causes people to misinterpret each other's claims. When you are speaking, try to be as clear as you can; and when you are listening, politely ask questions to resolve ambiguity and vagueness before making any (potentially false) assumptions.

Of course, people also like to play with ambiguity. Many jokes in newspaper comic strips exploit this awareness. For example, imagine a comic strip where, in the first panel, a man complains about his girlfriend's dog always getting in his way. In the second panel, he trips over the dog. In the third panel, we see him with two swollen black eyes, and he says, "I can't see you anymore." Was he being literal and telling her he could not physically see her any more? Or was he being figurative and ending their relationship? (Obviously, when the joke is explained like it was just now, it isn't all that funny!)

2.4 Emotion and Prejudice

As mentioned at the beginning of this chapter, the connotation of a word is the positive or negative emotional associations that are connected with it. Depending on which emotional button you are trying to push, you may refer to another person as a vagrant or homeless, shy or withdrawn, boisterous or loud. It is best to use **neutral language** when presenting an argument, since the focus should be on what your words denote and not their associations.

Neutral Language: Phrasing that does not carry positive or negative connotations.

Language with overtly strong emotional associations tends to show up in emotionally charged contexts. In the classic horror film *Halloween*, a young man who is suffering from a mental illness kills a few teenagers. Now, if you were one of the characters in the film and were being chased by this fellow, who is exhibiting certain severe anti-social tendencies, you might not use the terms "mentally ill" or "insane" but instead scream, "Help! There's a guy who's after me and he's nuts, demented, disturbed, sick, unbalanced, unhinged, certifiable, deranged, a lunatic, and a crazed maniac!" Clearly, you are very emotional (understandably so) and have a very negative view about the young man, and such words help make your point. You are using **emotionally charged language** that gives the listener a strong sense of your views. But in the academic world, and in day-to-day life, when you are discussing an issue that deals with mentally ill individuals, such emotive terms are completely unnecessary and unacceptable.

If you go to the other extreme and play down the undesirability of events by using bland and obtuse terms, known as **euphemisms**, this too can be a problem. Waterboarding is torture, so don't just call it an "enhanced interrogation technique." The killer in *Halloween* is most accurately described as "psychopathic," not "emotionally disturbed." Don't mislead your audience. Tell it like it is with neutral language. Don't use bias or overly emotionally loaded terms to stir up inappropriate feelings, but also don't use euphemisms that make very serious situations sound far less so.

Still, it must be mentioned that euphemisms and emotionally charged language do have an appropriate use outside of arguments. North Americans tend to refer to the use of the toilet with euphemisms such as "nature calls" or "restroom break," and there's nothing wrong with this, as it is polite and doesn't obscure meaning.

Prejudicial language occurs when you use words that contain or reflect bias. Consider the following two statements:

He was insulted.

He claims he was insulted.

While the second statement is not all that different from the first, inserting the phrase "he claims" suggests that there is some doubt as to whether the person was actually insulted. Prejudicial language can also come about through the manner in which you vocally express certain terms.

He *says* he was insulted.

This sentence is identical to the preceding one, except that it emphasizes the word "says," either through italics or through verbal intonation. By drawing attention to the word, the sentence suggests that the speaker is lying.

Emotionally Charged Language: Language that conveys a strong positive or negative feeling or mood.

Euphemism: A word or expression that is used in place of a more direct expression so as to avoid negative connotations.

Prejudicial Language: The use of biased terminology or vocal intonation to indicate or hint at personal feelings or opinions about the value, truth, or falsehood of the claim being made.

2.5 Scope and Conviction

When assessing the merits of any argument, you need to check for presentation consistency. That is, you need to see if the person has created an argument that uses words and phrases that are appropriate and used uniformly throughout. For example, consider the **scope** of a statement. *Scope is the number of members of a group that are being referred to.* A statement might use words such as "most," "some," "all," "three," "a handful," "a vast majority," and so forth, all of which express some degree of scope. What you want to be aware of is that "most Albertans" implies a *broader* scope than "some Albertans," and "a few Maritimers" implies a *narrower* scope than "some Maritimers." A statement with the broadest possible scope, covering *all* members of a group, is called a *universal statement*; "All trees have branches" and "Every computer contains a hard drive" are examples of universal statements.

Because scope is important, you need to ensure that it is consistently maintained throughout the argument. In general, the broader the scope, the easier it is for someone to defeat the argument. Suppose that Cameron and Dieter are discussing how there seem to be a lot of famous comedians from Canada (e.g., Jim Carrey, John Candy, Russell Peters, Dave Foley, Seth Rogen, Catherine O'Hara, and on and on). If Cameron claimed that this was because "All Canadians are funny," Dieter could **refute** this universal claim very easily by finding just one example of a Canadian who is not funny. Whereas if Cameron applied a narrower scope and stated, "Some Canadians are funny," then when Dieter identified a Canadian who is not funny, this would not be problematic for Cameron. Scope that does not include or exclude all members of a group allows the arguer some wiggle room. Even though Dieter found a Canadian who isn't funny, Cameron's claim is still safe. After all, she didn't claim that there aren't *any* Canadians who aren't funny!

The degree of **conviction** that a person has regarding the truth of the claims that he or she makes is also important since it can affect the outcome of his or her argument. **Unqualified statements** *are statements that convey certainty about what is true.* Examples of unqualified statements include "Tomorrow *it will definitely* rain," "Disneyland *is* the happiest place on the planet," "Tomorrow *it will definitely not* rain," and "Disneyland *is not* the happiest place on the planet." To be unqualified, a statement need not be true; all that matters is the strength of conviction of the person making the statement. You might claim that you are 100 per cent certain that Toronto is the centre of the universe. It isn't. You might be willing to bet that Superman is purely an American superhero, but in fact he was co-created by Toronto-born artist Joe Shuster. Statements such as "There are UFOs," "I am the tallest person in the city," and "*Beyond any shadow of doubt* ghosts really exist" are all unqualified, even though they are clearly controversial—if not blatantly false.

A **qualified statement** backs down from an apparent guarantee of knowledge. Instead of the rather paranoid statement "*I know for certain* that everyone

Scope: The number or proportion of members of a group that a statement is referring to. A statement's scope may be narrow or broad.

Refute: To demonstrate that a statement is false.

Conviction: The degree of confidence conveyed by a statement.

Unqualified Statement: A statement that conveys certainty about what is true. For example, "It will definitely snow this weekend."

Qualified Statement: A statement that does not convey certainty about what is true. Identified by such expressions as "It might be true that...."

is talking about me," the speaker can offer a qualified statement such as "*I think* everyone is talking about me," "Everyone is *probably* talking about me," "It could be the case that everyone is talking about me," or even "I'm not sure but there might be a possibility that everyone is talking about me." Here, the individual's conviction is tempered with a bit of possible doubt.

It is quite common to combine limitations on scope and conviction in your arguments. You could say, "There's a possibility (qualified claim) that a few people (narrow scope) are talking about me." Recognizing what is at play here is imperative because the more qualified the statement, the less justification is required. If you just want to say, "There might be a God," then the evidence required to support this is going to be less than that required for the claim that "There is a God." There is a danger, however, when you start qualifying your statements. The more you qualify your statements, the less powerful they become. For example, the statement "It is perhaps the case that God might exist" is uninteresting. With such weak claims, instead of starting an interesting discussion, you wind up having colleagues shrugging their shoulders and saying "Yeah, so what?" It's important not to make unqualified statements about things you're unsure of, but it's also important not to over-qualify and end up saying less than you want to.

2.6 Incorrect Word Choices

Your choice of words is important, and how you present these words can affect your audience's ability to understand your claims. Poor grammar, typographical errors, and sloppy sentence structure all get in the way of expressing yourself well. If readers have to work at figuring out what you are trying to say because of your errors or your use of slang or pretentious terminology, etc., then they may just become annoyed and focus on the wrong things. You want people to pay attention to the content of your message, not how poorly it is being presented. Here is a sampling of the most common word choice errors that people make:

Affect is most often a verb: Staying up late affected my ability to work well the next day.
Effect is most often a noun: Washing the car had a great effect on its appearance.

Can means something is possible: Can I go? Yes, you can walk, can't you?
May means you are permitted: May I go? No, you have homework to do first.

Could have/Would have are grammatically correct.
Could of/Would of are wrong.

Feel is a matter of sensations or emotions: I feel upset about the war.
Think is a matter of beliefs: I think that war is wrong.

i.e. is an abbreviation for the Latin words *id est*, meaning "that is." It is used to indicate an explanation, clarification, or definition.

e.g. means "for example."

Thus, you can say "I want to spend a lot of money (i.e., more than $100,000.00) on a fancy car (e.g., a BMW or Porsche)."

Its is a possessive: Please make sure you wash the car. Its windows need cleaning.

It's is a contraction of "it is" or "it has": It's true, she won!

Than is used in comparison statements: He is faster than you.

Then is used to refer to a different time or to indicate the order of events: He was faster back then. He used to be faster than you, but then he stopped training.

There is a location.

Their is a possessive.

They're is a contraction of "they are." Thus, you can say "They're there at their meeting."

Thing/word confusion: "Orange is black" is false but "'orange' is black" is true. In the first statement, "orange" refers to the *thing*—the fruit. In the second statement, "orange" is in quotation marks and so it refers to the *word* "orange"—which is black because the print on this page is black.

Whose is a possessive: Whose car is that?

Who's is a contraction of "who is": Who's coming over for dinner?

Your is a possessive: Your car is dirty.

You're is a contraction of "you are": You're coming over tonight, right?

2.7 Chapter Exercises

Exercise 2.1

TRUE/FALSE QUESTIONS

1. If a definition is too broad, the definition includes items that are not normally referred to by the word defined. True or False?
2. If we defined "argument" as "a violent disagreement," this definition would be too narrow. True or False?
3. "Because people are different in many ways, they are not the same; and because they are not the same, they are not equal. Therefore, equality between people does not exist." This argument depends on the ambiguous use of the word "same." True or False?
4. It is always wrong to use emotionally charged language. True or False?
5. "This toaster is completely free; you just have to pay for shipping and handling and the membership fees." This is an example of vague language. True or False?

Exercise 2.2

QUESTIONS ABOUT DEFINITIONS

1. "Doll" is defined as "a toy for children." What is wrong with this definition?
2. "Woman" is defined as "a female mammal." What is wrong with this definition?
3. "Gloves" are defined as "protective covering of the hands used during winter." What is wrong with this definition?
4. "Justice" is defined as "fairness." What is wrong with this definition?
5. Which of the following words can be easily understood by means of an ostensive definition? How would you provide this definition?
   a. Friend
   b. Sneeze
   c. Cold
   d. Entertainment
   e. Dream
   f. Bright

Exercise 2.3

Open a dictionary at any page and see if you agree with the definitions provided. Are any of them too broad, too narrow, circular, or obscure?

Exercise 2.4

Read the letters to the editor or advertisements in your local newspaper and identify all the examples of emotionally charged terms you can find. In each case, offer a neutral word that means the same thing. Compare your examples with those of a colleague.

Exercise 2.5

Find two newspapers (or television news broadcasts) that discuss the same event. Compare and contrast the descriptions. Are there any differences in the reporting or comments made about the event? Do the reports contain different emotionally charged terms or prejudicial language?

Exercise 2.6

Study the lyrics of one of your favourite songs. How many different examples of concepts discussed in this chapter can you find (e.g., positive and negative connotations, vagueness, ambiguity, etc.)?

Exercise 2.7

Put the following statements in order from least specific (i.e., most vague) to most specific.

1. a. Tuition costs have changed this year.
   b. Tuition rose 130 per cent over last year.
   c. Tuition has increased.
   d. Tuition has more than doubled.

2. a. James and Jane decided to spend their summer holidays in Spain.
   b. James and Jane discussed their summer plans.
   c. James and Jane talked about the coming summer.
   d. James and Jane tossed around some ideas.

3. a. The wind storm caused a lot of damage to the campus.
   b. The wind storm could have been worse.
   c. The wind storm caused around $50,000 in damage on campus.
   d. The wind storm was pretty strong.

4. a. The student was late to class because it took her longer than usual to get there.
   b. The student was late to class because she got a flat tire and had to take the bus.
   c. The student was late to class because she didn't make it on time.
   d. The student was late to class because she couldn't take her car.

2.8 Postscript

As we have noted, it's important to understand *what* a person is telling you before you start arguing with him or her. For this reason, you should seek out acceptable and mutually agreed-upon definitions for any terms that you're using. While some of the misuses of language that we have seen in this chapter may be considered appropriate within certain contexts (e.g., it is acceptable to use a euphemism in order to be polite), we must be on guard for when people use euphemisms, vagueness, ambiguities, and emotionally charged language to mislead. We should always strive to use clear and neutral language in argumentation so that others can focus on the content of our claims and not on their manner of delivery.

CHAPTER 3
Argument Structure and Assessment

One of the things you learned from the first chapter is that when you are evaluating an argument you cannot simply state, "this is a good argument." That is an unsupported claim, and it will not convince anyone of anything other than the fact that the speaker has a particular belief. When evaluating an argument you have to defend your response—meaning you need to offer an argument in return. But there are a few steps that you need to take first before you evaluate an argument:

1. Identify that you are dealing with an argument and not some other form of expression or communication. (See Chapter 1 for a discussion of how to identify arguments.)
2. Read the argument a few times to be sure you understand it completely. (See Chapter 2 for some of the uses and abuses of language to watch out for during this step.)
3. Standardize the argument, with the premises coming before the conclusion. This can involve
   - editing the argument carefully to omit excess and unnecessary information that is not an element of the argument. This includes editing out any jokes, digressions, and introductory or background remarks, then determining if there are missing premises or conclusion(s) and adding them.
   - figuring out how the premises connect to the conclusion(s) and organizing the statements in their logical order.

53

This chapter focuses on Step 3. We'll also look briefly at the basics of argument evaluation, as it's important to have some sense of how arguments are evaluated in order to properly standardize and edit them.

3.1 Standardizing Arguments

Standardization:

The rewriting of an argument by identifying and labelling its premises and conclusion(s). This is done in order to see the logical flow of the argument.

After you have determined that you are actually dealing with an argument, you must standardize it. **Standardization** allows you to have a visual representation of the argument such that each premise and conclusion is clearly demarcated. Even though the conclusion is sometimes the very first thing people offer—e.g., "Taking a vacation is a good idea *because* it helps people relax"—*the logical structure of an argument always moves from the premises to the conclusion.* Thus, no matter where the conclusion is in the original passage, it will always appear at the end of your standardization.

Here are two versions of the same argument. Although the premises and the conclusion are identical, they appear in different order. Nevertheless, you will notice that the *logical* structure is the same in each passage.

> Version 1: I believe that all animals originated from chickens because every animal that I have eaten tastes like chicken, and if it tastes like chicken, then it is chicken.

> Version 2: Every animal I have eaten tastes like chicken. Therefore, all animals originated from chickens since if it tastes like chicken, then it is chicken.

Version 1 with indicator words CAPITALIZED and the parts of the argument in *italics*:

> *<Conclusion>* I believe that all animals originated from chickens BECAUSE *<Premise>* every animal that I have eaten tastes like chicken, and *<Premise>* if it tastes like chicken, then it is chicken.

Version 2 with indicator words CAPITALIZED and the parts of the argument in *italics*:

> *<Premise>* Every animal I have eaten tastes like chicken. *<Conclusion>* THEREFORE, all animals originated from chickens SINCE *<Premise>* if it tastes like chicken, then it is chicken.

If you were to standardize either of these two versions so that the logical structure is evident you would see this:

> Premise 1) Every animal I have eaten tastes like chicken.
> Premise 2) If it tastes like chicken, then it is chicken.
>
> Conclusion 3) Therefore, all animals originated from chickens.

When standardizing, write out each distinct statement (i.e., each premise and the conclusion) on a separate line. Do not just write out the sentences, since one sentence might contain more than one discrete idea. The conclusion of the argument will be the last statement in your standardization regardless of where it appears in the original passage. No matter whether there is a conclusion indicator or not, use the conclusion indicator word "therefore."

Next, number each statement in order (1, 2, 3, 4, and so forth). Then add the labels "Premise" (or "P") and "Conclusion" (or "C") where appropriate.

Let's try another example:

There is no milk at home and I need milk for the baby, so I will have to go to the store.

First, write out each statement of the argument:

There is no milk at home.
I need milk for the baby.
Therefore, I will have to go to the store.

Then number the statements in their logical order:

1. There is no milk at home.
2. I need milk for the baby.
3. Therefore, I will have to go to the store.

After you have numbered the statements, go back, identify and label the premises and conclusions. Thus, the last statement of this argument is labelled C3 because it is a conclusion and it is the third statement in the standardized argument. Draw a line between the premises and the conclusion to give a greater sense of visual separation.

P1) There is no milk at home.
P2) I need milk for the baby.
———————
C3) Therefore, I will have to go to the store.

Finally, compare the standardized argument with the original argument to ensure that the intent of the original argument has not been altered.

3.2 Editing Arguments

When we make arguments in speech or in writing, we often add extraneous details that have no bearing on what's argued. When standardizing an argument, it is sometimes necessary to remove or slightly rephrase sentences to ensure that the standardization includes only the information needed to assess the argument itself.

Consider the following:

As usual, I was reading the morning newspaper, and I saw—I think it was on page 3—that the prime minister's poll numbers are up. I think that means he'll probably call an election soon.

In this passage the information about the person's reading habits and what particular page the article was on is not relevant to the argument. It is all background. It has no influence on whether or not the argument is ultimately persuasive. (Still, it should be noted that the name of the particular newspaper *may* be relevant if, for example, the newspaper is one that is known for inaccurate reporting. That is, if the news was reported in a sensationalist tabloid, the accuracy of the information could be called into question.)

So the proper standardization of the above argument is:

P1) The prime minister's party's poll numbers are up.

C2) Therefore, he'll probably call an election soon.

During standardization, omitting unnecessary information also means deleting premise indicators. While it can be helpful to include the conclusion indicator, the premise indicators are unnecessary. In fact, if you did include them, the statements would not be standardized in proper English.

Consider this argument:

Since the stores will be closed tomorrow and because I don't have any milk at home, I believe I need to go shopping today.

It would be wrong to include the premise indicators, since the statements would then not make sense as independent sentences and so could not be judged true or false.

P1) Since the stores will be closed tomorrow.
P2) Because I don't have any milk at home.

C3) Therefore, I believe I need to go shopping today.

"Since the stores will be closed tomorrow" and "Because I don't have any milk at home" are incomplete sentences. If you said something like this, the listener would be waiting for you to finish your thought. Furthermore, it is not necessary to include the phrase "I believe" since it is self-evident that this is already what the arguer believes.

The proper standardization would be:

P1) The stores will be closed tomorrow.
P2) I don't have any milk at home.

C3) Therefore, I need to go shopping today.

More on Editing Arguments

1. Replace pronouns such as "me," "they," "we," etc. even if it is obvious who or what the pronouns are referring to.

   Wrong: "They went to the store." Who is "they"? Without context, this is vague.
   Right: "Rosina and Kathi went to the store." No context is needed. It is now clear who went.

   (Obviously if you do not know who "they" is referring to, just leave the pronoun in. You would not be justified in inserting any name that you liked.)

2. Change any rhetorical questions into proper true or false statements. If the original says, "Who wouldn't want lower taxes!?," the standardized version should just be "We all want lower taxes."

3. Exclamation points should be removed. All propositions should be written with the use of a period. "Shouting" your message does not make it any stronger. Be calm and reasonable. You are arguing, not fighting.

4. Be sure not to add any information that is not included in the original argument. If no names were included in the argument, don't add any names. And if the original argument said "Some dogs are omnivores," don't change it to "All dogs are omnivores" or "Most dogs are omnivores," even if you know this is true. Conclusion indicators can be added because they only indicate the form of the argument and don't add any additional information.

3.3 Reconstructing Arguments

The remainder of this book will be dedicated to showing you how to evaluate and create arguments, but in this chapter you just have to focus on learning the proper structure of standardized arguments. For you to fully understand how to standardize arguments, however, it might be helpful to understand the basics of the next step: argument evaluation. Here is an overview of the evaluation process that you will be using once you have standardized an argument. We will return to this process, which we call the **S-Test**, in greater detail in the next chapter.

The S-Test

1. To evaluate someone's argument, you must first consider each and every premise separately and then draw a conclusion about each one of them. That is, you must determine whether each premise is

S-Test: A means of evaluating an argument, according to which certain conditions must be met in order for the argument to be successful. These conditions are satisfactory premises that offer sufficient support for the conclusion.

Satisfactory Premise:
A premise that is true or that there is good reason to believe is true.

Supportive Premise:
A premise that is included in a given argument and suggests that the argument's conclusion should be accepted.

Sufficiency of Support: When an argument's premises provide enough support for its conclusion such that, if its premises are satisfactory, acceptance of its conclusion is rational.

satisfactory and then defend your answer. A premise is satisfactory if we have good reason to believe that it is true. Some premises are obviously satisfactory ("The sun will rise tomorrow"); others are obviously unsatisfactory ("The average human is nine feet tall"). In many cases it is not obvious whether or not a premise is satisfactory ("It will rain tomorrow" or "Alien life exists," for example) and so further investigation or argument is required.

2. After you have determined the (un)satisfactoriness of each premise, you must examine the connection between the premises and the conclusion. You need to ask, "Would the premises, if they were true, offer any **support** that would help establish the conclusion?" That is, do the premises, if true, provide any reason to believe that the conclusion is also true? The premise "All dinosaurs are dangerous" *does* support the conclusion "The stegosaurus is dangerous," but it *doesn't* support the conclusion "The woolly mammoth is dangerous."

3. If the premises do support the conclusion, you then need to determine if the premises, when taken together as a whole, offer **sufficient** support to establish the conclusion. If there is some evidence to establish the conclusion, is there enough evidence? If, for example, I say that "I've seen five swans, and they were all white," my claim *supports* the conclusion that "All swans are white," but it is not *sufficient* support, because I've only seen a very small number of swans.

These three S-words—Satisfactory, Sufficient, and Support—are the keys to the S-Test, and we'll examine each in greater detail in later chapters. Only if there is *sufficient support* for the conclusion and only if the premises are *satisfactory* may you ultimately conclude that an argument is successful. And if it is successful, then its conclusion should be accepted.

Let's try applying the S-Test to a simple example:

P1) Every Canadian province has a capital city.
P2) Manitoba is a Canadian province

C3) Therefore, Manitoba has a capital city.

First, look at each premise and ask whether it is *satisfactory*, that is, ask whether we have reason to believe that it is true. In this case, we all know that P1 and P2 are true, and so the premises are satisfactory. If you had some doubt, you might consult a reliable reference source such as the website of the Canadian government or an encyclopedia.

Now ask whether the premises *support* the conclusion. Indeed, if every Canadian province has a capital, and Manitoba is a Canadian province, then Manitoba must have a capital. Therefore, the premises do offer support.

Finally, ask whether the premises offer *sufficient* support for the conclusion. It's clear that they do in this case. In fact, the conclusion of this argument *must* be true given the truth of its premises. So this argument passes all three steps of the S-Test and is therefore a good argument.

Here's a slight variation on the above:

P1) Every Canadian province has a capital city.
P2) Manitoba is a Canadian province.

C3) Therefore, Winnipeg is the capital of Manitoba.

This argument has the same premises as the earlier one, and we already know that those premises are *satisfactory*. But do they provide *sufficient support* for the conclusion? No, they don't. They only indicate that Manitoba has a capital, not that the capital is Winnipeg. And so the argument fails the S-Test. Note that the argument fails *even though the conclusion is true*. When we apply the S-Test, we're only trying to determine whether the premises of the argument add up to show the truth of the conclusion, not whether the conclusion is independently true or whether some other argument might succeed in proving the conclusion.

Now that you know roughly what we're looking for when we evaluate an argument, let's look at some different argument types to see how we can most effectively standardize and interpret them.

Independent and Dependent Premises

It is usually the case that the more reasons you can provide for your conclusion the better. In arguments with **independent premises**, each premise by itself supports the conclusion. The greater the number of satisfactory independent premises you have, the stronger the argument becomes. For example, imagine you are trying to decide what apartment to move into. You might note the following:

P1) The apartment is close to the university.
P2) The apartment is quiet.
P3) The apartment is inexpensive.
P4) The apartment is clean.
P5) The apartment has a nice view.

C6) Therefore, I should rent this apartment.

Each premise offers a separate and unrelated reason for renting the apartment. If you only had one of these premises, it probably would not be enough to make you want to choose this apartment over some other one. That is, if the only reason you had was "the apartment is clean," this would not be sufficient for you to want to move in. What if the rent is too expensive? What if it is quite far from the university? Since independent premises provide independent reasons, each premise must be assessed individually.

Independent Premises: Premises that independently support the conclusion; each premise offers some degree of separate support for the truth of the conclusion.

Suppose that you are trying to decide whether to ask someone to marry you. The fact that the other person is breathing is a good reason, but it may not be a sufficient reason for you to commit the rest of your life to him or her. You need other independent reasons as well. For instance, that the person loves you back might be something you would want to consider. That the other person is kind, considerate, funny, smart, and thoughtful may be essential for you too. If one of these characteristics was removed, would your desire to marry the person be weakened? Maybe. Maybe not. True, some of the characteristics might be more important than others, so it might depend upon which reason was removed. But if two or three were removed, would your judgement that he or she is "the one" still stand? Probably not. So, the more independently satisfactory premises you have, the better off your argument will be (and the happier you will be too).

Dependent Premises: Premises that work together to establish a conclusion (and so should be evaluated together). Removing one of the premises creates a logical gap.

Dependent premises work together to support the conclusion. Thus, you want to *examine them all together* to assess their ability to offer support. Consider the following argument made by a record executive:

P1) Listening to this song, I can tell immediately that it will either be a huge success or an utter failure.

P2) The song will not be a huge success.

C3) Therefore, it will be an utter failure.

Imagine if the second premise was missing:

P1) Listening to this song, I can tell immediately that it will either be a huge success or an utter failure.

C2) Therefore, it will be an utter failure.

In the second argument, the record executive has given two possibilities (huge success or utter failure) and then has somehow decided that the song will utterly fail. But how does the executive know this? Without the second premise there is no justification to draw the conclusion. This helps us identify the fact that the record executive is using dependent premises. Imagine now that the first premise is missing:

P1) The song will not be a huge success.

C2) Therefore, it will be an utter failure.

You are now told the song will not be a huge success. But does this necessarily mean that it will be an utter failure? Surely not. Perhaps the song will become a minor hit or only a minor failure. What this shows is that the record executive needs to present both premises in order to justify the conclusion. In such arguments the premises fit together like links in a chain. Each depends upon the other(s) to maintain the chain. Each one needs the others to establish the conclusion. If one of the links was removed, there would be a logical gap and the chain of reasoning (pun intended) would be broken. We'll further examine the ways in which an argument's premises and conclusion can be linked together in later chapters.

Note that some arguments contain both independent and dependent premises. In these cases, the dependent premises work together to provide a reason in support of the conclusion, while each of the independent premises separately provides a reason in support of the conclusion.

Example of an argument with dependent premises:

P1) The Green Party candidate got 1,000 votes.
P2) You must get at least 2,000 votes to get elected.
_____
C3) Therefore, the Green Party candidate did not get elected.

Example of an argument with independent premises:

P1) The goldfish is a small fish.
P2) The goldfish is quiet.
P3) The goldfish is easy to take care of.
P4) The goldfish can be easily replaced with another if it dies.
_____
C5) Therefore, the goldfish might be a suitable pet for young children.

Example of an argument with both dependent and independent premises:

P1) Driving a car produces more CO_2 emissions than riding a bicycle. (dependent)
P2) CO_2 emissions are harmful to the environment. (dependent)
P3) Riding a bicycle is better exercise than driving a car. (independent)
P4) Riding a bicycle is less expensive than driving a car. (independent)
_____
C5) Therefore, you should ride a bicycle rather than drive a car.

Complex Arguments

When you are reading an essay or participating in a discussion, simple arguments can become complex fast. If a person offers premises that he or she thinks are satisfactory and sufficient, this does not automatically entail that the reader or listener will agree. In such cases further arguments may be needed to defend those premises, meaning that the entire argument may require multiple conclusions. For example, imagine the following conversation:

Andreas: Big box retailers are just not good for small cities.
Barbara: Why not?
Andreas: Because they drive out the competition.
Barbara: How so?
Andreas: Big box retailers can order large quantities at significantly reduced prices. Small local stores can't match these low prices, so many will go out of business.

As well, wages at these big box retailers are usually only the minimum that is allowed by law.

Here is the standardized version of Andreas's argument. First the distinct statements are identified and then numbered. The premises and conclusions are then labelled with P (for Premise) or C (for Conclusion).

P1) Big box retailers can order large quantities at significantly reduced prices.

P2) Small local stores can't match these low prices

_____

C3) Therefore, many small local stores will go out of business.

_____

C4) Therefore, big box retailers will drive away competition.

P5) Wages at these big box retailers are usually only the minimum allowed by law.

_____

C6) Therefore, big box retailers are just not good for cities.

Whole Argument: The entirety of premises and conclusions (including any sub-arguments) that make up an argument.

Sub-argument: An argument provided to establish a statement that is then in turn used as a premise to justify another conclusion within a complex argument.

Intermediate Conclusion: A statement that is the conclusion of a sub-argument and is used as a premise for another conclusion within a complex argument.

Main Conclusion: The foremost "idea" or "point" in an argument; the statement that the argument's premises and sub-arguments are ultimately meant to support.

Complex Argument: An argument that includes at least one sub-argument.

We call the entire set of statements, from P1 to C6, the **whole argument**. You can see that premises P1 and P2 are used to support C3. Even though Andreas's third statement is a conclusion and is labelled as such, it is also used as a premise for C4. C4 is then used in combination with P5 for establishing C6. Statements P1 to C3 are referred to as a **sub-argument**, and the conclusions C3 and C4 are referred to as the **intermediate conclusions**. Intermediate conclusions are also used as premises to try and establish what is to come. Although Andreas has tried to support the intermediate conclusions (which is why they are labelled with a C and not a P), they are not the **main conclusion**, the primary point that the argument is meant to establish. Any argument that contains sub-arguments is called a **complex argument**.

Since it was not obvious to Barbara why Andreas believes what he initially put forward, Andreas attempted to provide further support to establish statements 3 and 4. He then used these along with premise 5 to support the conclusion 6. In other words, Andreas's statement became complex in response to Barbara's questioning.

If Barbara found flaws along the way in Andreas's argument, she would point these out, and Andreas would have to either add more evidence to convince Barbara or admit that the whole argument is unsuccessful. Please keep in mind that it is not Barbara's responsibility to fix what is broken; to evaluate the argument, she only needs to point out its flaws. Then, if she so desires, she can offer her own views.

If you were asked to evaluate Andreas's first sub-argument, you would do it in the following manner.

1. Evaluate the satisfactoriness of P1.
2. Evaluate the satisfactoriness of P2.
3. See if P1 and P2 offer any support for C3. If not, then the sub-argument P1 to C3 fails.

4. If P1 and P2 do offer some support, then see if they are also sufficient for establishing C3. If they are sufficient for establishing C3, then you have a good sub-argument. If they are not, then the sub-argument fails.

Important Note: Even if the sub-argument fails, the whole argument may still succeed in establishing the main conclusion. Consider:

I have a Great Dane named George. Therefore, a lack of sleep can prolong minor illnesses. So it is important to get plenty of rest when you have a cold.

This argument is standardized as follows:

P1) I have a Great Dane named George.
_____

C2) Therefore, a lack of sleep can prolong minor illnesses.
_____

C3) Therefore, it is important to get plenty of rest when you have a cold

Normally, you would first determine whether P1 is satisfactory, but let's skip that step in this case. Ask whether P1 is relevant to the intermediate conclusion C2. In this example, P1 offers no support to C2 because it is completely irrelevant (not to mention being a rather odd thing to say given the other statements). There is no connection between having a dog and the effects of lack of sleep. So the sub-argument fails. However, the intermediate conclusion C2 is nonetheless true, and it is sufficiently supportive of the argument's main conclusion, C3. In other words, though the sub-argument fails, the whole argument still succeeds because it offers sufficient support for the main conclusion.

Go back to Andreas's argument and look at it again. Suppose that P1 and P2 are *not* satisfactory. If so, then the sub-argument for C3 fails. But C3 may nonetheless be true and therefore satisfactory. If C3 is satisfactory, then you should ask whether it is sufficiently supportive of C4. If it is, then the sub-argument for C4 succeeds, and the final step of the argument, from C4 and P5 to C6, can be assessed for sufficient support. The bottom line is that a complex argument shouldn't be thrown out altogether if one of its sub-arguments fails; rather, you should ask whether the sub-argument's conclusion is nonetheless satisfactory and sufficiently supportive of the conclusion it is being used to establish.

Missing Premises and Conclusions

Consider the following argument:

She is a good companion. Therefore, I should marry her.

How is it possible that the premise supports the conclusion? There is an implicit or **missing premise** here that connects the premise with the conclusion. It is clear that the arguer links being a good companion with being a candidate for marriage. Thus, the missing premise is something like "I should marry someone who is a

Missing Premise: A premise that is unstated but is required by the logical form of the argument.

good companion." When reconstructing this argument, we can add the missing premise because it is implied in the original passage. So, in this case, the standardized argument looks like this:

P1) She is a good companion.
MP2) I should marry someone who is a good companion.
_____
C3) Therefore, I should marry her.

The "M" in "MP2" stands for "Missing."

Now suppose the arguer put forward something slightly different:

She is wealthy. Therefore, I should marry her.

Here the arguer is linking wealth to marriage, so the missing premise is "I should marry someone who is wealthy," and the reconstructed argument goes like this:

P1) She is wealthy.
MP2) I should marry someone who is wealthy.
_____
C3) Therefore, I should marry her.

But is this enough to fully understand the arguer's reasoning? It is sometimes difficult (though not always impossible) to reconstruct a person's reasoning process when they leave out information. How is wealth a sufficient reason to marry someone?

When adding missing premises, you can only work with what is logically necessary to move from the premise to the conclusion. It is not appropriate to make up anything that you think might fit. Thus, for this case the only premise you can add is P2, which directly links being wealthy with being suitable for marriage, even if you don't think it is true. You may be tempted to add additional premises such as "Wealthy people are good companions" or perhaps "Wealthy people will always make their spouses toast on Sundays, and I like toast." But if you do this, then you are no longer reconstructing the original argument but instead creating your own argument. You cannot provide any more details since you are not given any.

How would you reconstruct the following argument:

My brother is a doctor; therefore, he is very intelligent.

The conclusion indicator "therefore" shows that the first part of the sentence is a premise and the second part is a conclusion.

P1) My brother is a doctor.
MP2) ?
_____
C3) Therefore, my brother is very intelligent.

It's obvious that a missing premise is needed here. But what exactly is the link? Which of the following missing premises makes the best connection?

1. Most doctors are very intelligent.
2. A few doctors are very intelligent.
3. Anyone who is in my family is quite intelligent.
4. Doctors are intelligent.
5. All doctors are very intelligent.

Missing premise 1 is incorrect because the scope of "most doctors" is too narrow, given that the conviction in the conclusion is strongly stated. It states without qualification that "my brother is quite intelligent," so if the scope of the missing premise were just "most," then it might not include "my brother." For the same reason, premise 2, "a few," is far too narrow. If only a few doctors are very intelligent, then there would be stronger evidence to argue the opposite, namely, that "my brother" might *not* be intelligent.

Missing premise 3 is just plain silly. Don't add statements to another person's argument that you know would not be claimed by that person. The goal is to capture the original argument, so give the arguer the benefit of doubt and assume that they wouldn't make absurd claims unless such claims are logically required in order to connect the premises to the conclusion.

Missing premise 4 is not the best answer because the term "doctor" could be interpreted as referring to all doctors or just some doctors—it is not clear which is intended. This is why when you mean "All X's are Y," you should say exactly that and not just "X's are Y." Otherwise, if you claimed that "birds are black" or "dogs are mammals" another person might interpret your claim to be about *all* birds and *all* dogs or only *some* birds and *some* dogs.

Also, note that in missing premise 4 the word "intelligent" is not the same as "very intelligent." When adding missing statements, make sure that you *capture all and only what the arguer has provided.* Leaving out or changing a word here or there makes a big difference. Compare the short phrase "Your cat is friendly" with "Your cat is *extremely* friendly" or "I like you" versus "I love you."

The right premise to add has to be the last one, number 5. "All doctors are very intelligent."

P1) My brother is a doctor.
MP2) All doctors are very intelligent.
———————————————
C3) Therefore, my brother is very intelligent.

The scope covers all individual doctors and matches the unqualified nature of the conclusion. The premises of this reconstructed argument also sufficiently support the argument's conclusion; of course, whether they are satisfactory or not is a different question.

Missing Conclusion:
A conclusion that is unstated but is required by the logical form of the argument.

Some arguments aren't missing any premises but have a **missing conclusion**. For example, here's an argument that might be given by an advertiser: "You like insanely high levels of caffeine and Brand X energy drink is insanely high in caffeine!!!" Here, the advertiser wants you to draw the conclusion for yourself. It is obvious what the conclusion is supposed to be: "You should buy Brand X energy drink." When standardized, the argument appears as follows:

P1) You like insanely high levels of caffeine.
P2) Brand X energy drink is insanely high in caffeine.

MC3) Therefore, you should buy Brand X energy drink.

This method of leaving out information forces the other person (in this example, the potential consumer) to draw the conclusion that the arguer intends him or her to draw.

When you are standardizing an argument and you believe there is a logical gap that is evident due to a missing premise or conclusion, you must supply it. This is because the claim is actually "there" but just not made explicit. If you think there are more than one or two missing propositions, then there is likely something seriously wrong with either your interpretation of the argument or the argument itself.

If you suspect that there is an implicit or missing statement that has not been provided, you should look at the flow of the argument and ask yourself, "What is the connection between these statements? How did the arguer move from point A to point C?" In the case of a missing conclusion, ask, "What follows from these statements? What are they meant to establish?" Be careful not to change the original meaning of the argument. Paying attention to the scope and the degree of conviction can help. Only use the information provided and do not add too much!

In some cases, when you don't see the connection between the dependent premise(s) and the conclusion, you need to determine if there really is a connection or if the person has just "jumped" to a conclusion that is simply unwarranted. Consider the following argument:

3D televisions are not selling as well as manufacturers had hoped. So now is the time to buy a new TV!

The conclusion indicator "so" makes it clear that the second sentence is the argument's conclusion, but the link between the first sentence and the second is not obvious. What is the reasoning here? Perhaps the argument is this:

P1) 3D televisions are not selling as well as manufacturers had hoped.
MP2) If 3D televisions aren't selling well, they must be going down in price.

C3) Therefore, now is the time to buy a new TV.

Or perhaps the argument is this:

P1) 3D televisions are not selling as well as manufacturers had hoped.
MP2) We should support the television manufacturing industry.
_____
C3) Therefore, now is the time to buy a new TV.

Or even this:

P1) 3D televisions are not selling as well as manufacturers had hoped.
MP2) If 3D televisions aren't selling well, then they won't likely be supported in the future.
MP3) If 3D televisions aren't likely to be supported in the future, you might as well buy the non-3D television you've had your eyes on.
_____
C4) Therefore, now is the time to buy a new TV.

You may think one or another of these arguments is more plausible. However, the original passage doesn't include enough information to determine which was intended, and we cannot add the missing premises unless we're sure that they were implied. The only acceptable missing premise would be something like "If 3D televisions are not selling as well as manufacturers had hoped, then now is . the time to buy a new TV"—but this wouldn't help the argument make any more sense, so it's not really necessary to add. If the arguer is present, we might ask, "What do you mean?" or "What is your reasoning?" But until those questions are answered, the argument is best left as it is.

There are a number of reasons why a person might leave a premise or a conclusion out of his or her argument, including:

1. *The arguer may not see any need, due to context.* For example, Erica and Fred are discussing a government initiative to offer subsidies to multinational corporations if they expand their operations to other Canadian provinces rather than moving overseas. The government has decided that job creation is both necessary and the best way to stimulate economic growth. Erica is arguing that the government is right while Fred disagrees. Erica says, "It is important that people have jobs to create greater disposable income. This puts money back into the marketplace." Fred might respond by claiming that "Jobs are not enough to get the economy running well again. The national debt has to be tackled first." The missing conclusions of Fred and Erica's arguments are obvious from the context of the conversation and need not be restated.

2. *Leaving missing premises or conclusions unstated may lead to more engaging conversation or writing.* When you are constructing your own arguments, the omission of obvious premises or conclusions can be used to draw another person in and lead them to actively follow

your reasoning as a partner rather than as an opponent. For example, suppose Dawn says to Justin, "The movie was really suspenseful—I was on the edge of my seat the whole time! I think you'd really like it." Dawn could spell out her belief that Justin likes suspenseful movies, but this missing premise is already obvious from what she's said. Leaving it unspoken sounds less awkward and may compel Justin to engage with Dawn's reasoning about his preferences.

3. *In some cases, leaving out premises or conclusions may be more polite.* For example, if you don't want to hurt someone's feelings by coming right out and saying that you don't want to go out with them, you might honestly tell them, "Right now, I'm really only interested in dating someone that I can see myself with in the long run. Sorry!" Here, the missing premise (that you can't see yourself with this person in the long run) and the missing conclusion (that you won't date this person) are excluded so as to be less hurtful. Of course, in this case, you run the risk that your listener will draw the opposite conclusion!

4. *The premise or conclusion may have been defended already or raised elsewhere.* Suppose you are having a discussion with a colleague and she says, "Dogs are good pets, so you should get a dog." The missing premise here may be something that you and your colleague have already discussed and agreed on. Perhaps you were talking earlier in the week about getting a pet or you were saying you didn't like coming home from work to an empty house and wanted some company, so your colleague has built that bit of knowledge into her argument.

3.4 Chapter Exercises

Exercise 3.1

TRUE/FALSE QUESTIONS

1. If you deleted an independent premise from a good argument, the conclusion would no longer follow from the remaining premises. True or False?

2. When we compare the statements "All dancers are fit" and "Many dancers are fit," we see that the scope of the second statement is narrower than that of the first. True or False?

3. Consider this passage: "Jim probably won't leave his apartment today, because of the blizzard outside. So he'll likely just stay on his computer and surf the Internet." The passage contains a sub-argument. True or False?

4. Consider this argument: "Tree bark is a natural substance, therefore it is safe to eat." The missing premise is "It is safe to consume anything that is natural." True or False?

5. In the argument "If I can hear the neighbours, then the walls are too thin. I can hear them." The missing conclusion is that "Neighbours should be quiet and respect others." True or False?

Exercise 3.2

1. Create an argument that counters Andreas's main conclusion regarding the impact of big box stores. Switch your answer with a colleague and informally assess the merits of your colleague's argument.
2. Create a complex argument that supports either Erica's or Fred's position regarding government subsidies for multinational corporations, then discuss and compare your argument with a colleague's.

Exercise 3.3

Find a commercial (on television or online) that makes an argument and write out the argument that is being used to sell you the product. How easy is it to determine what the premises and conclusion are? Are there any missing statements? Do any of the images shown play the role of a missing statement?

Exercise 3.4

Interpret each of the following passages as an argument, and determine what the missing premises or conclusions are in each case. Standardize your answers and be sure to label correctly.

1. I will burn my tongue if it is hot. OUCH! I burnt it!
2. Either it will be sunny today or it will rain and I will get wet. I guess when I get home tonight I will have to change out of my soaked clothes.
3. All polar bears wear toques. Here's a polar bear.
4. What is that over there? Well, if it is a spider, then you will hear me scream in a minute. Ah, see, I didn't scream!

Exercise 3.5

Determine whether the following arguments have dependent or independent premises. Try standardizing them as well.

1. The weather was fine, the people were friendly, the music was nice, and the food was great. All in all, it was a good day.
2. You stumble when you walk; you mumble; you don't talk; you seem not to notice that your right arm is at an unnatural angle; and apparently you are attracted to my brain and not my beauty. You must be a zombie.
3. If they don't finish the voting recount soon, we won't know who won until tomorrow. What? They are finished counting? Yay!

4. We will only know if you are allergic to the food after you eat it. Okay, so you only had one bite and now you're covered in hives? I guess you must be allergic!

5. According to the local media, the tax increase will be beneficial for a variety of reasons. It will help offset any environmental costs, it will help fix the bridges, and it will provide the government officials with a nice pension.

3.5 Postscript

In this chapter, we examined the structure of arguments, including how to reconstruct an argument in a standardized form so that it can be evaluated. We looked briefly at the S-Test, as it is necessary to have some knowledge of how argument evaluation works in order to properly standardize arguments and charitably insert missing premises and conclusions. But we've not yet looked at it in enough detail to effectively apply it to a wide range of arguments. In the following chapters, we'll examine the S-Test more thoroughly, and we'll see how it applies to the many different types of arguments that we regularly encounter.

Please don't worry if the sample arguments discussed above scare or confuse you. It is a lot of information to absorb at once. Just recall how terrifying it was slipping behind the steering wheel of a car for the first time. There was so much to look at and remember: the buttons, the dials, the signs on the street, the traffic, the intersections, the pedestrians, and on and on and on. And now? Now you don't even think about it. You just get in the car and drive.

CHAPTER 4
Argument Evaluation

In the previous chapter, we discussed how to standardize arguments. Now, we will focus on the stage that comes next: argument evaluation. We have already briefly outlined the S-Test, a series of three steps that you can follow to evaluate any argument. Recall the three steps:

1. Determine whether the argument's premises are *satisfactory* (that is, whether we have good reason to believe that the premises are true).
2. Determine whether the premises *support* the conclusion.
3. Determine whether the premises offer *sufficient* support to establish the conclusion.

An argument that passes all three steps of the S-Test is a good argument; an argument that fails any step is a bad argument. We'll now look at each step in detail.

4.1 Step 1: Satisfactory Premises

The first step is to examine the satisfactoriness of each premise. Typically we say that the premises are satisfactory when we have good reason to believe that they are true.

In some cases, it's obvious whether or not a premise is satisfactory. In other cases, it's not obvious at all. There are no hard and fast rules for the evaluation of premises; Step 1 may require research, calculation, or common sense. Literally any statement can be a premise, and knowing whether or not a given statement is reasonable to believe may require experience and contextual knowledge. It would be impossible here to address *all* of the possible reasons why we might believe a premise to be true, but let's look briefly at a few common criteria.

Expert Authority

Relevant Expert:
An honest and reliable expert in a given area. A statement that is the shared opinion of relevant experts is usually satisfactory when used as a premise in an argument.

Premises are generally satisfactory when **relevant experts** support them. It makes sense to seek the advice of a medical professional for a health concern, and it makes sense to seek the advice of a mechanic for an automotive problem because both are authorities in their respective fields. However, not just any expert will do. You wouldn't take your car to your medical doctor, nor would you take your health problem to your mechanic.

The proper authority must be (a) an expert, (b) an expert in the relevant area, (c) honest and reliable (or at least there should not be any reasonable evidence suggesting the contrary), and (d) in agreement with other experts in the area regarding the claim at issue. Regarding this last point, have you noticed how in a court case the defence and the prosecution can each separately call their own expert witnesses? No one is accusing the experts of purposely lying, but if two experts can't agree on the truth of a statement, then we have no reason to believe one expert rather than the other. We can only say that a premise is satisfactory due to expert authority if experts generally agree about what is being stated. Thus, when you are provided with only one person's expert belief, it is sometimes valuable to seek out a second, and a third, and so on.

A few examples of statements that appeal to proper authority:

Almost all doctors agree that a low resting heart rate is a sign of good health.

My mechanic, and the three other mechanics I consulted, all tell me that my transmission needs to be replaced.

The consensus among philosophy professors is that George Berkeley was an empiricist.

Each of these statements appeals to a proper authority, and so when these statements are used as premises in arguments, they are most likely satisfactory. Remember, though, that these claims are only satisfactory if they are in fact the opinions of the experts mentioned—*do* almost all doctors really agree that a low resting heart rate is a sign of good health? You may have to do some research to determine whether this is so.

Common Knowledge:
Any statement that is commonly known to be true. What constitutes "common knowledge" depends on the audience being addressed.

Common Knowledge

Some premises are satisfactory because they are **common knowledge**. Don't confuse common knowledge with the "commonsense" beliefs discussed in Chapter 1. Common knowledge does not include unwarranted beliefs and superstitions. Rather, common knowledge is just the shared knowledge that is presupposed as background to an argument; premises that are common knowledge don't need to be thoroughly investigated because they are obviously true. Keep in mind, however, that you must be careful when classifying something as "common knowledge"—historically, many supposedly obvious "truths" have turned out to be false, and we've all had the experience of discovering that we were mistaken about something that we thought we *knew*.

We have all learned many things from what we have read, seen, experienced, and been taught. If you *know* something, that means it *must* be true. However, *you should not confuse knowing something with believing something*. You probably know how old you are, what your name is, and where you live. If you merely *believe* something, your belief may be true or it may be false. Have you ever believed it was Tuesday when in fact it was Monday, or gotten the time wrong, or been mistaken about someone's name? You believe many, many things, some of which are true and some of which are false.

People who buy lottery tickets may believe they will win, but most won't win the big jackpot. The people who lost who believed they would win had *false beliefs*. Moreover, given the odds of winning, even the person who actually did win was not warranted in that belief. Suppose that Leigh won even though the odds were against her. Accordingly, her belief that she would win was true, but she was not justified in believing it. If she had used her belief as a premise in an argument (say, to convince herself that she should buy a lottery ticket), it would have been an unsatisfactory premise—even though she ended up winning!

Here are some examples of statements that we would all count as common knowledge and which are thus satisfactory premises when used in an argument:

Toronto is in Canada.

Humans cannot survive without water.

Some people enjoy eating pizza cold.

Personal Testimony

Premises are usually satisfactory when they are reports based on personal experiences. This only applies if the person offering the report is honest and reliable; at a minimum, there should be no evidence to make you doubt that he or she is honest and reliable. Sara tells you what she did on the weekend. She tells you what book she read, what movie she saw, what she had for dinner, and so forth. There is no reason to doubt her. However, it's still possible that her report is false. This wouldn't necessarily mean that she is lying to you on purpose (although she could be)—she might just be mistaken. Think about what you did on November 29 last year. Think about what you did last month or even yesterday. Are you sure of what you did? Probably not; this is why even honest and sincere eyewitness accounts are notably problematic in a court of law.

Personal testimony is satisfactory when the claim made is plausible and restricted to the individual's personal experience. It is fine to believe Simon's account of seeing an eagle soaring above the river. But if he says he saw 10,000 eagles at once, this would require further investigation. Ten thousand? Really? That many? Has this sort of event ever happened before? Is there someone else who can back this claim up? Perhaps he was exaggerating for effect. Suppose that his exact words were "I saw *a lot* of eagles, there must have been 10,000 of them!" In this case, while the exaggerated number helps give you a picture of what Simon witnessed, the claim is obviously an embellishment and not meant to be a realistic or accurate report, even though Simon is in general an honest and reliable person.

Pay attention to word choice. For example, it is not appropriate to accept someone's claim that he or she saw a ghost, because this would require acceptance of the general claim that ghosts exist and (at best) no one knows if ghosts exist. But you could accept the claim if the person qualified it by stating, "I *believe* I saw a ghost" or "I saw something that looked like a ghost." You can accept these claims as satisfactory without accepting anything about ghosts being real.

Here are some other examples of statements based on personal testimony:

I heard a loud crackling sound five minutes ago.

Omar says that his favourite kind of pizza is pepperoni.

Zoe claims that she's never been to an NHL hockey game.

Unless we have reason to doubt the honesty or reliability of those giving the reports, we should treat these as satisfactory premises when they are used in an argument.

Unverifiable Premises

Before moving on, let's address a special kind of premise. There are some arguments in which the truth or falsity of the premises cannot, in principle, be verified. For example, how do you know that you are not dreaming? What proof do you have? You cannot simply rely on the inference that, since you are reading this book, you must be awake—perhaps you are just having a really, really boring dream. Whether other people possess minds or feel pain is not easily demonstrable either. Perhaps there is no real world "out there," or perhaps there is no one besides you and everything else is just a figment of your imagination. Indeed, even things in the past are difficult to verify. Try to prove that there was (or was not) a red flower in bloom on June 15 in the year 1428 in what is now the province of Quebec. These sorts of concerns are not just word games but are philosophically important since they raise questions about existence and knowledge. Still, outside the confines of your philosophy classroom, it's not normally necessary to

---

Personal Testimony:
A statement made by an individual about his or her own personal experience. Usually, personal testimony is satisfactory when the claim is plausible and the person is not known to be dishonest or unreliable.

question the unverifiable assumptions about the nature of reality that we normally take for granted. So, in most cases, you can assume that the world and the other people in it aren't just figments of your imagination without further argument.

However, some unverifiable claims are not so obviously satisfactory. Moral claims, in particular, are usually difficult or impossible to verify, and they arise frequently in arguments. Statements about what is of value or about what one ought to do are moral claims. In some cases, such claims are entirely uncontentious and are therefore satisfactory. "Torture is a bad thing" and "Freedom is better than slavery" are uncontentious and wouldn't normally require any defence. In other cases, moral claims may indeed require some further argument. "Stealing is wrong" may be true in most cases but may also admit of exceptions (if one is starving, for example); "A welfare state is better than a free market" may seem obviously true to some people but obviously false to others. If statements like these are used as premises in arguments, they will not be satisfactory unless some further arguments are provided. That's not to say that these statements *cannot* be true; whether a moral claim can be true is one of the classical questions of philosophy. But if any particular moral claim is not obviously true, then we cannot assume that it is satisfactory.

If an argument includes a moral premise that can't be verified, you might go on with the rest of the S-Test and then, if the argument passes the other steps of the test, explain that its conclusion depends on the truth of its moral premise. Suppose that you are evaluating the following argument:

P1) Using animals to test cosmetic products is always immoral.
P2) Smoothskin Makeup tests its cosmetic products on animals.

C3) Therefore, Smoothskin Makeup's testing processes are immoral.

P1 may be true or it may be false, but it's not a claim about which there is universal agreement, and in this context no further argument in its support has been provided. Yet, if we proceed with Steps 2 and 3 of the S-Test, we find that this argument's premises do indeed offer sufficient support for its conclusion. So, when assessing this argument, we might say that "*If* P1 is true, *then* C3 is true as well." Though this is less cut and dry than cases in which an argument clearly passes or fails the S-Test, it's sometimes the best we can do when working with unverifiable moral premises.

4.2 Step 2: Supporting Premises

The relationship between an argument's premises and its conclusion(s) is extremely important. Step 2 of the S-Test is determining whether the premises provide some degree of support for the conclusion. *Questions about satisfactoriness are separate from questions of support*—satisfactory premises can still make a failed argument if they don't support the conclusion. Support is determined by **relevance**. If your

Relevant Premise: A premise that is included in a given argument (or sub-argument) and has bearing on whether the argument's conclusion should be accepted.

conclusion is that you should wear a t-shirt and shorts today, a good reason—that is, a premise that would support your conclusion—would be that it is warm outside. The temperature of the air *is* relevant to what sort of clothing you should wear. On the other hand, the fact that you have an exam today is *irrelevant* to the truth of your conclusion and so offers no support.

Irrelevant Premise: A premise that is included in a given argument but has no bearing on whether the argument's conclusion should be accepted.

Statement A is relevant to statement B if A's being true has any effect on whether or not we should think that B is true. This means that, technically, A is relevant to B if A supports B *or* if A suggests that B is not the case. Let's say that A is "I am rich" and B is "I can buy an expensive car." The truth of A supports the truth of B (if I know that you are rich, then I have reason to believe that you can buy an expensive car), so A is **positively relevant** to B. But also notice that if A is "I am not rich," it is *still* relevant to B because the truth of A affects how we should assess the truth of B ("I can buy an expensive car"). In the second case, A is a reason why we should think that B is *not* true—it is **negatively relevant**. Although, technically speaking, relevance can be either positive or negative, it's normally sufficient to interpret "relevance" in the positive sense; in most cases, "relevant" can be taken as shorthand for "positively relevant."

Positively Relevant Premise: A premise that is included in a given argument and suggests that the argument's conclusion should be accepted.

Step 2 of the S-Test requires that we look at each *independent premise* separately to determine whether each independently supports the conclusion. In the case of *dependent premises*, however, you should assess them together to see if, taken together, they provide support for the conclusion.

Negatively Relevant Premise: A premise that is included in a given argument and suggests that the argument's conclusion should not be accepted.

Imagine you are investigating a homicide and have a suspect. In order to get a court order to arrest the person, you need to provide some evidence that the suspect is guilty.

> Police Officer: We think Jeff is the murderer.
> Judge: Why?
> Police Officer: Because his fingerprints were found on a bottle of red wine near the victim's apartment.
> Judge: That doesn't suggest that he's a murderer.
> Police Officer: The bottle was broken.
> Judge: How is that relevant? Maybe he dropped the bottle.
> Police Officer: Maybe. But the victim had shards of glass and traces of red wine in his hair.

Each of these premises (that the bottle had Jeff's fingerprints, that the bottle was broken, and that the victim's hair contained glass and wine), *on its own* would fail to indicate that Jeff is the murderer. That is, the statements would not offer support if treated as independent premises. But if we treat them instead as dependent premises and examine them together, we can see that they do indeed support the conclusion.

Keep in mind that even though the premises are relevant to the conclusion, the evidence could be false. The evidence could have been planted, or there could have been an error in the fingerprint analysis. Yet, even if the premises are false, they would support the conclusion *if* they were true. This is why checking the satisfactoriness of the premises is separate from and independent of checking to see if they are relevant to the conclusion.

Consider this old joke, paraphrased from the *Pink Panther* movie with Peter Sellers:

(Sue is walking down the street and encounters Tony and a small dog.)
Sue: Is your dog friendly?
Tony: Oh yes.
(Sue reaches down to pet the dog; the dog snarls and bites Sue's finger.)
Sue: Ouch! I thought you said your dog was friendly!
Tony: I did. That's not my dog.

If the dog was Tony's, then it would be friendly; this is true. However, the assumption made by Sue, namely, that this particular dog was Tony's, is false. Tony's response was satisfactory in the sense that his dog (but not the dog that is with him) is friendly. Yet that response does not support Sue's conclusion that it would be safe to pet the dog; the premise regarding Tony's dog was entirely irrelevant.

Most of the time, all of an argument's premises must offer support for the conclusion in order for the argument to succeed. Suppose I offer you the following argument:

P1) The apartment has an en suite washer-dryer.
P2) It's also pet friendly.

C3) Therefore, you should rent the apartment.

If you happen to desire the features mentioned in P1 and P2, then both premises are supportive. But suppose you don't like pets, and so P2 has no bearing on your decision. In that case, only one of the two premises offers support, and so only that premise can be taken into account when assessing sufficiency of support (in Step 3 of the S-Test), and the argument is thus likely to fail. On the other hand, if I had instead listed a dozen reasons why you should rent the apartment (e.g., it's a great location, the rent is low, it has a nice view ...), and all of those other reasons were relevant to your decision, then the argument might succeed even though P2 doesn't offer any support. Remember, though, that only the premises that *do* offer support can be included when applying the third step of the S-Test.

4.3 Step 3: Sufficient Support

Returning to the murder investigation, once you collect *some evidence* to arrest Jeff on suspicion of murder, you need to collect *enough evidence* to prove him guilty of the crime. So, if the discussion continued, you might hear the introduction of new details:

Police: Not only do Jeff's fingerprints match those found on an apparent murder weapon, but there are 10 honest eye witnesses who saw him leaving the scene of the crime immediately afterwards. They all separately agree that his shirt was covered in blood.

Jeff sure looks guilty. The earlier evidence is of course relevant but probably not enough for a conviction. However, that evidence combined with the eye witness accounts may be sufficient support to establish the conclusion that he is guilty.

In a successful argument, the premises must supply sufficient support for one to rationally accept the conclusion. In order to determine whether the support is sufficient, you need to apply your knowledge of the various concepts we have discussed to this point. Look at the scope of the statements to see if the scope of the conclusion is warranted by the scope of the premises, and consider whether the premises are persuasive enough to justify the degree of conviction shown in the conclusion. The next chapter will explain in more detail how to evaluate sufficiency of support in specific types of arguments.

4.4 Passing the S-Test

So, to sum up once again, this is how to evaluate arguments:

1. *Satisfactoriness.* Check the satisfactoriness of each premise separately. Is each premise either certainly true or at least reasonable to believe?
2. *Support.* Check whether the premises offer some support for the conclusion. If they are independent premises, examine them separately; if they are dependent premises, look at them all together. If none of the premises offer support, the argument fails Step 2 and obviously cannot pass Step 3 (because you cannot have sufficient support if you have no support!). If there is some support, move on to Step 3.
3. *Sufficient Support.* Check whether, when taken together, the premises supply enough support to justify the conclusion.

Successful Argument:
An argument in which the premises are satisfactory and sufficiently support the conclusion.

A **successful argument** must pass all three steps: Satisfactoriness, Some Support, and finally Sufficient Support equals Success!

Note that it can be instructive to move on to Steps 2 and 3 of the S-Test even when an argument fails Step 1. Of course, if the premises fail to be satisfactory, you know that the argument is not going to work, but it is useful to appreciate the whole argumentative process so that each element can be discussed and fixed if necessary.

4.5 Failing the S-Test

Failing Satisfactoriness

The following argument fails Step 1 of the S-Test:

P1) Everything is either expensive or shiny.

P2) Blue jeans are not expensive.

C3) Therefore, blue jeans are shiny.

P1 is unsatisfactory because it is obviously false. A clump of dirt is neither expensive nor shiny. P2 is unsatisfactory because it is vague. How much is "not expensive"? Not expensive for whom? And the scope is also unclear: does it mean just *some* blue jeans or *all* blue jeans?

Even though the two premises are unsatisfactory and so you know the argument is not going to work, it would pass the second and third steps of the S-Test: the premises offer some support to the conclusion, and that support is sufficient. *If* the premises were true, the conclusion would have to follow.

The following examples show some—but not all—of the reasons why you might reject a premise as unsatisfactory.

Premises are unsatisfactory when you can refute them by means of **counter-examples**. For example:

> Premise: All birds fly.
> Problem: A penguin is a bird and it can't fly, so the premise is clearly false.

As discussed in Chapter 2, a counter-example is effective against a universal statement, such as "People *never* do ...," "People *always* do ...," "*All* people do ...," or "*No one* does ..." One merely needs to provide a single counter-example to prove these statements wrong. Thus, against the claim that people never do X, you need only give an example of one person who does do X; when the claim is everyone does X, you need only find one person who doesn't do X.

Premises are unsatisfactory when you can refute them using an acceptable *appeal to testimony*:

> Premise: Robert stayed home yesterday.
> Problem: Your best friend says she saw Robert at the theatre yesterday.

Or *authority*:

> Premise: Plato is known as "The Father of Modern Philosophy."
> Problem: Your philosophy instructor and the author of your philosophy text both state that what we know as "Modern Philosophy" began centuries after Plato died and that René Descartes is called "The Father of Modern Philosophy."

Counter-example: An example that refutes or contradicts a universal statement.

Or *common knowledge*:

> Premise: All birds are white.
> Problem: Anyone who has hiked or who has been to a pet store knows that birds come in many colours.

Or when their meaning is *vague*:

> Premise: I did okay on the test yesterday.
> Problem: This doesn't specify what you mean by "okay." Are you saying that you passed? That you did better than last time? That you received a "B"?

Or when they are *ambiguous*:

> Premise: I would be happy to give that person a ring tomorrow.
> Problem: It's not clear what this means. Are you planning on making a phone call or proposing?

If a premise is unsatisfactory, do not attempt to fix it yourself when you are standardizing it. If Simon actually claimed he saw 10,000 eagles, do not rewrite this as "He saw many eagles." Do not try to improve another person's argument on your own—that is the arguer's responsibility.

Failing to Support

Consider the following argument:

> P1) $2 + 2 = 4$
> P2) The moon is round.
> P3) Many people like chocolate.
> _____
> C4) Therefore, I should buy a new car.

All of the premises are satisfactory, yet none of them supply any support for the conclusion. Whether or not the premises are true has no bearing on the truth of the conclusion—the premises are *irrelevant*.

Not being able to supply any support, the premises cannot provide *sufficient* support either. Thus, this argument is unsuccessful because it fails Steps 2 and 3.

Consider also the following example:

> P1) Fast food is often very unhealthy.
> P2) I don't like fast food very much.
> _____
> C3) Therefore, I should have fast food for dinner tonight.

In this example, the premises are *negatively relevant*—instead of offering support for the conclusion, they suggest that we should *not* accept the conclusion. Since these premises don't support the conclusion at all, the argument is unsuccessful because it fails Step 2 (and therefore it also fails Step 3).

Failing to Sufficiently Support

P1) Some Canadians suffer health problems as a result of fast food consumption.

P2) Many fast food restaurants serve meals that are over the government recommended caloric intake for the average person.

P3) One role of government is to promote the welfare of citizens, including in matters of physical health.

_____

C4) Therefore, the government should force fast food restaurants to close down.

Here, the premises are commonly known to be true, so they are satisfactory. The premises offer some support for the conclusion, since, taken together, they offer reason(s) as to why the government should shut down fast food restaurants. However, the conclusion is too strong for the premises. In other words, the premises do not provide *sufficient* support for the conclusion. The argument passes Step 1 and Step 2 but fails Step 3. The premises *might* be sufficient if the conclusion was toned down to state, for example, that the government should encourage restaurants to provide healthy food options.

4.6 Chapter Exercises

Exercise 4.1

TRUE/FALSE QUESTIONS

1. If an argument's premises are all satisfactory and supportive of the conclusion, the argument must be successful. True or False?
2. "I have a dog" sufficiently supports the conclusion that "I like pets." True or False?
3. For a premise to be satisfactory, you must know for certain that it is true. True or False?
4. When an argument is good, it is called a "true argument." True or False?
5. If a premise is missing, the argument must fail. True or False?

Exercise 4.2

How satisfactory is your own personal testimony? What was your instructor wearing during the last class? What was the class about? Did it end early or late or right on time? Who sat in the front row? Now compare your answers with a colleague's.

Exercise 4.3

Write a successful argument that consists of two premises and one conclusion. Then write an unsuccessful argument for the same conclusion. Next, pass both versions to a colleague and see if he or she can figure out which argument passes and which fails the S-Test. Here are some sample conclusions, but you can choose any conclusion that you like (so long as it can be sufficiently supported by satisfactory premises):

Post-secondary students should travel overseas when they have finished their schooling.

Small companies should get tax breaks.

Unions are no longer necessary in business.

It is acceptable for advertisers to mislead viewers regarding their products.

All citizens have a right to universal health care.

Exercise 4.4

In the examples given below, does the first claim (A) support the second claim (B)? Is there an obvious missing premise that is needed in order for A to support B?

1. (A) All fish swim in the ocean. (B) The ocean may rise if more icebergs melt.
2. (A) Bears live in apartment buildings. (B) Bears are dangerous animals.
3. (A) At university there are many different courses in the humanities and the sciences. (B) Universities are a good place to learn new things.
4. (A) He is honest and reliable and is not prone to exaggerating. (B) He would make a good witness for the defence.
5. (A) Dreams are things that cannot be controlled. (B) Sometimes we experience things that we have no power over.
6. (A) Hockey players use sticks to move a puck around the ice. (B) Hockey players must not only be good at skating but also have good hand-eye coordination.
7. (A) Spaniels make nice family pets. (B) Dogs can be expensive to own.
8. (A) I enjoy playing football. (B) I enjoy watching movies too.
9. (A) If a man loves a woman, he should not tell her unless he wants to risk losing her as a friend. (B) People should always be honest with others.
10. (A) This blue car has some minor damage to it, but it is still roadworthy. (B) That red car is brand new and costs a lot.

Exercise 4.5

Determine whether the following statements are satisfactory or not. Defend your answers.

1. Some people enjoy listening to music while eating dinner.
2. According to my friend, who is a scientist, the planet Venus was created by the explosion of a much larger artificially created planet some 50,000 years ago.
3. I have tried three different brands of soap, and Spot-Be-Gone is the best one on the market today.
4. I saw a big man yesterday. He was huge.
5. You can catch sexually transmitted infections easily by swimming in a public pool.
6. Victor is blue.
7. I like birthday parties.

Exercise 4.6

Here are some additional arguments, some of which we considered earlier. Standardize the arguments and then determine which are successful using the S-Test. Be sure to defend your answers. Hint: some of these arguments have one or two missing statements.

1. Birds can fly. Bats can fly. I can fly. Therefore, all living things can fly.
2. All mammals have DNA. I am a mammal. Therefore, I have DNA.
3. Every day around noon, my boss has ordered the same thing for lunch. He always calls me to place the order for him. Let's see, it's almost noon now. So he will soon be calling me to place an order for his usual lunch.
4. Jazz is made up of complex arrangements, like classical music. Classical music has been around for centuries and has withstood the passage of time. I suspect jazz will do the same.
5. I have 2,000 comic books in my basement and 4,000 more in my study. I also have 50 locked away in my safe. So I have 6,050 comic books in total.
6. I was watching the local newscast last night and the meteorologist was reporting that the weather along the East Coast has been much more dramatic these past years. She said that every year there have been more storms than the year before and the storms have been stronger than ever. Given that it's almost winter, I guess the people living along the East Coast should expect there to be some strong storms, over and above what they have experienced in the last few years.
7. Most people need regular exercise to stay healthy as they get older. Well, you're no longer young! Cycling is a great way to exercise, so you should give it a try if you want to stay healthy.

8. As far as I can tell based upon your stupid actions, your brain is about the size of a dinosaur's. They didn't manage to live that long, so I think you better smarten up.
9. I have a bag of different coloured marbles. Ten are black and two are red. With my eyes closed, I just removed a red marble from the bag; so, the next one I remove will probably be black.

Exercise 4.7

Randomly select one option from each of columns a, b, c, and d to create a conclusion that starts with "It is." Then randomly select an option from e and attempt to make an argument either for or against your conclusion that meets the conditions stated in e. Be sure to try a few different ones, since there are 7,500 possible combinations! Feel free to make a game out of this exercise by putting the different column letters on scraps of paper and shuffle them like cards.

STATEMENT GENERATOR: MORAL ISSUES

		a	b		c	d	e
1	It is	Always	Obligatory	for	Adults	To do something risky for the benefit of others.	Unsatisfactory premises. No support for conclusion.
2		Usually	Right		Children	To do something selfish that could harm others.	Unsatisfactory premises. Some support, but not sufficient support for conclusion.
3		Sometimes	Permissible		Community members	To get on a bus without paying the fare.	Unsatisfactory premises. Sufficient support for conclusion.
4		Hardly ever	Wrong		Family members	To do something illegal if they know they will never be caught.	Satisfactory Premises. No support for conclusion.
5		Never	Prohibited		Friends	To keep a friend's secret even if it hurts someone else.	Satisfactory premises. Some support, but not sufficient support for conclusion.
6						To have a same-sex relationship.	Satisfactory premises. Sufficient support for conclusion: successful argument.
7						To buy unnecessary expensive electronic gadgets even though there are children starving in the world.	
8						To wear products made from animals.	
9						To sell their own kidneys.	
10						To download music from the Internet without permission from the copyright holders.	

Now do the same exercise with some statements from business contexts.

STATEMENT GENERATOR: BUSINESS ISSUES

		a	b		c	d	e
1	It is	Always	Obligatory	for	CEOs	To use insider information.	Unsatisfactory premises. No support for conclusion.
2		Usually	Right		Bosses	To be more loyal to the public's concerns than the company's.	Unsatisfactory premises. Some support. Not sufficient support for conclusion.
3		Sometimes	Permissible		Employees	To take credit for the work of subordinates.	Unsatisfactory premises. Some support, but not sufficient support for conclusion.
4		Hardly ever	Wrong		Family members	To do community charity work only if it helps the company.	Satisfactory premises. No support for conclusion.
5		Never	Prohibited		Friends	To not have expense accounts checked.	Satisfactory premises. Some support. Not sufficient support for conclusion.
6						To be monitored at work.	Satisfactory premises. Some support, but not sufficient support for conclusion.
7						To take drug tests for employment.	Satisfactory premises. Sufficient support for conclusion: successful argument.
8						To date others from the office.	
9						To get more from society than they put into it.	
10						To increase the safety of a product even though it will significantly increase cost.	

4.7 Postscript

The S-Test is appropriate for the assessment of any argument, whether it has dozens of premises and multiple sub-conclusions or a single premise and a single conclusion, whether it deals with an abstract philosophical subject or with mundane everyday events. In some cases, application of the three steps of the S-Test is straightforward and obvious; in other cases, any or all of the steps may be exceptionally tricky.

As you may have noticed while considering the above examples, arguments also differ in the strength of their conclusions: some aim to show the truth of a conclusion beyond any doubt, while others aim to show only that a conclusion is probably true. These different types of arguments require different standards for sufficient support. In the next chapter, we will discuss the basic argument types and how the S-Test applies to each of them.

CHAPTER 5
Argument Types

Arguments come in different "flavours," and there are three that you will come across most often: deductive arguments, inductive arguments, and arguments from analogy.

This chapter will show you how to identify and understand these basic types of argument and give you some language to use when evaluating them. We will also discuss ways to apply the general strategy of the S-Test to each specific type. Knowing the argument type is especially helpful for the last step of the S-Test, since different kinds of argument differ in their standards of sufficient support—deductive arguments require a greater degree of support than inductive arguments do.

5.1 Deductive Arguments

A person who offers a **deductive argument** aims at achieving *certainty*; in a successful deductive argument, the conclusion *necessarily* follows from the premises, and the premises are true.

P1) All cats meow.
P2) Sam is a cat.
_____
C3) Therefore, Sam must meow.

If the premises of this argument are true, the conclusion *must* be true as well. *If* Sam is in fact a cat, and *if* it is true that all cats meow, then it *must* be true that

Deductive Argument:
An argument in which the premises are intended to provide a guarantee of the truth of the conclusion.

Inductive Argument: An argument in which the premises are intended to provide a high degree of probability that the conclusion is true.

Sam meows. If Sam doesn't meow, then you can be sure that at least one of the argument's two premises is false.

5.2 Inductive Arguments

When one offers an **inductive argument** one tries to establish a reasonably high level of *probability*. That is, while the premises do not guarantee the truth of the conclusion, they still (if true) give you a strong case for accepting it.

P1) The vast majority of the students in the class like drinking coffee in the morning.

P2) You are a student in the class.

C3) Therefore, you probably like drinking coffee in the morning.

Argument from Analogy: An argument that draws a conclusion about one case (called the "primary subject") on the basis of its similarities to another case (called the "analogue").

Primary Subject: In an argument by analogy, the subject of the conclusion.

5.3 Arguments from Analogy

Arguments from analogy *draw comparisons* between different cases. If the two cases have enough relevant similarities, then our conclusions about one case should apply to the other case as well.

P1) The doctor told Julian that he needs to get more exercise because he's out of shape.

P2) Rebecca is out of shape as well.

C3) Therefore, the doctor would probably also tell Rebecca to get more exercise.

Analogue: What the primary subject is being compared to in an argument from analogy.

In arguments from analogy, the topic of the conclusion is referred to as the **primary subject**. In the above case, Rebecca is the primary subject. This is being compared to the **analogue**: Julian.

Most arguments from analogy, including the one above, are inductive—they establish a probable (but not certain) conclusion. However, some of the techniques we use to assess arguments from analogy are unique, and so we'll treat this category separately in this chapter.

Valid Argument: A deductive argument in which the premises necessarily lead to the conclusion; that is, it is impossible for the argument's premises to be true AND its conclusion to be false. If it is possible for the premises of the deductive argument to be true AND the conclusion to be false, the argument is invalid.

5.4 Evaluating Deductive Arguments

A deductive argument aims to establish its conclusion with certainty. A good deductive argument must first be **valid**. *A valid argument is one in which it is impossible for the premises to be true and the conclusion false.* Validity has nothing to do with whether the premises are *in fact* true. To test for validity, what you want to do is look at the premises and ask, "Are there any possible circumstances in which the premises could be true and the conclusion false?" If the answer is "No," then the argument is valid. If the answer is "Yes," then it is invalid.

Consider:

P1) All dogs are mammals. (True)

P2) All mammals are warm-blooded. (True)
_____

C3) Therefore, all dogs are warm-blooded. (True)

It would be impossible for the conclusion to be false if the premises are true (and they are), so this is a deductively valid argument.

If the conclusion was instead "All dogs are friendly," then it would be a deductively invalid argument, as the conclusion would not follow from the premises; that is, the premises could be true and the conclusion false. So the following example is invalid and thus unsuccessful:

P1) All dogs are mammals. (True)

P2) All mammals are warm-blooded. (True)
_____

C3) Therefore, all dogs are friendly. (False)

Remember, the premises don't have to be true for the argument to be valid. Validity is only concerned with an argument's logical structure, not its content. So you could make up something inane but valid like this:

P1) If I had three hands, I could scratch my back, your back, and your friend's back all at the same time.

P2) I do have three hands.
_____

C3) Therefore, I can scratch my back, your back, and your friend's back all at the same time.

The second premise of this argument is obviously false. But the argument is still valid, since *if the premises were true*, the conclusion would also have to be true.

Because we don't need to know the truth of an argument's premises in order to assess its validity, we can even check the validity of arguments in which we're uncertain whether the premises are true. Consider:

P1) If I don't find a job, my children will go hungry.

P2) If my children go hungry, then I will have to give them over to government services.
_____

C3) Therefore, if I don't find a job, I will have to give my children over to government services.

These premises *may* be true, but they're hypothetical and difficult to assess. Maybe my children will go hungry if I don't find a job, or maybe I could feed them adequately through employment insurance or donations from the food bank.

Regardless, if the premises were true, the conclusion would have to be true, and so this argument is valid.

Indeed, when it comes to validity, you may not even need to know the meaning of the premises if you can see the argument's logical form. This argument is deductively valid:

P1) All X's are Y's.
P2) All Y's are Z's.
_____
C3) Therefore, all X's are Z's.

Whatever X and Y and Z are, the conclusion has to follow from the premises. If, however, the conclusion was "Therefore, no X's are Z's," the conclusion could be false with the premises remaining true. Accordingly, the argument wouldn't work. It would be invalid. Now see what happens when you make X = mothers, Y = female, and Z = people who have given birth; or X = fish, Y = things that live in water, and Z = things that are wet.

Ultimately, when assessing deductive arguments, we wish to know not just whether they are valid but whether they are **sound**. A sound deductive argument is one that *is valid and has only true premises*. Thus, an argument can be valid and unsound, but a sound argument cannot be invalid.

Sound Argument: A deductive argument that is valid and has only true premises.

Here is the most famous example of a sound deductive argument:

P1) All humans are mortal.
P2) Socrates is human.
_____
C3) Therefore, Socrates is mortal.

The conclusion here *must* be true. The argument is obviously valid, as there is no way to dispute its conclusion once its premises have been established. Furthermore, its premises are in fact true, and so it is sound. Given that all humans are in fact mortal and given that Socrates is human, Socrates *must* be mortal.

Here's an argument that is valid but unsound (because the first premise is false):

P1) If vegetables don't scream when you pull them out of the ground, then this is only because they are too shocked by the event to say anything.
P2) Vegetables don't scream when you pull them out of the ground.
_____
C3) Therefore, they must be too shocked to say anything.

Now here are some other very simple deductively sound arguments.

P1) All Pacific Salmon swim.
P2) No butterflies can swim.
_____
C3) Therefore, no Pacific Salmon are butterflies.

P1) If the sentence is written in English, then it is not written in French.
P2) The sentence is written in English.

_____

C3) Therefore, it is not written in French.

P1) You are either alive or dead, not both.
P2) You are alive.

_____

C3) Therefore, you are not dead.

Each of these arguments has true premises and a conclusion that follows with certainty from those premises. If you accept that an argument is deductively sound, then you cannot rationally reject its conclusion because the conclusion has been established with certainty.

Deductive Arguments and the S-Test

Because a deductive argument attempts to show that its conclusion is certain, the standard for sufficiency of support is very high: support is only sufficient if the premises *necessarily* lead to the conclusion—meaning that, if the premises were true, the conclusion would absolutely have to be true as well.

Apply the S-Test to a deductive argument as follows:

1. *Satisfactoriness*: Is there good reason to believe that the premises are true? If not, the argument fails the S-Test and is not sound, but it may still be valid.
2. *Support*: Are the premises relevant to the conclusion? If not, the argument fails the S-Test and can be neither sound nor valid.
3. *Sufficient Support*: Is it impossible for the premises to be true and the conclusion false? If so, the argument is valid. If not, the argument fails the S-Test and can be neither sound nor valid.

If the argument passes all three steps of the S-Test, it is sound.

5.5 Evaluating Inductive Arguments

Inductive arguments are used for scientific predictions, historical claims, forecasts, and probability assertions, among other things. The premises of an inductive argument do not guarantee the truth of its conclusion; rather, inductive arguments deal with probabilities, such as the following:

It was hotter all this week than last. Summer may be finally here.

Seventy per cent of the students did well on the test; therefore, you probably did well too.

Whenever I turn on my computer with that new game installed, it crashes. I bet it will crash the next time too!

When you ate that much candy last Halloween, you got sick. So please don't do it again this year, okay?

Inductive arguments can draw general conclusions based on specific premises:

The first time we played, she beat me 8-6. The second time it was 10-5. Then she beat me 7-5, 9-6, 6-0 (specific examples). Therefore, I foresee that she will continue to beat me unless I improve my game (generalization).

They can also be used to draw specific conclusions based upon general premises:

You probably just have the flu (specific conclusion) because most of my patients who have been here this week have it (generalization).

Inductive arguments are assessed in terms of how much support the premises give to the conclusion and whether the premises are acceptable. *An inductive argument is traditionally evaluated as either strong—if it shows that the conclusion is very likely—or weak—if it doesn't.* Here is a strong inductive argument:

Strong Inductive Argument: An inductive argument that successfully shows that its conclusion is highly likely.

P1) Almost all dogs are friendly.
P2) Here is a dog.
_____
C3) Therefore, this dog is probably friendly.

Weak Inductive Argument: An inductive argument that fails to show that its conclusion is highly likely.

Notice in this example that the conclusion has been qualified (i.e., "is probably friendly" as opposed to "will certainly be friendly" or just "is friendly"). This is because the scope of the first premise, while broad, does not include all dogs, so there is a possibility that the dog in the argument is not friendly. However, rationally speaking, the odds are such that you could go up and play with this dog and need not be afraid of it. It will probably lick your hand, but there's still a slim chance it will bite it instead!

Inductive Arguments and the S-Test

Because an inductive argument attempts to show that a conclusion is probable (instead of certain), the standard for sufficiency of support is not as high as it is for deductive arguments—support is sufficient if the premises give us enough reason to think that the conclusion is likely to be true.

Apply the S-Test to an inductive argument as follows:

1. *Satisfactoriness*: Is there good reason to believe that the premises are true? If not, the argument fails the S-Test and is weak.
2. *Support*: Are the premises relevant to the conclusion? If not, the argument fails the S-Test and is weak.

3. *Sufficient Support:* Do the premises offer enough support to justify the strength of the conclusion? (If the argument uses statistics, consider elements such as the size of the sample and whether the sample was representative; we'll discuss the evaluation of statistics in more detail below.) If the premises don't offer enough support, the argument fails the S-Test and is weak.

The Problem of Induction

Inductive arguments are often (but not always) used to *predict how the world will be* tomorrow based on the regularities that were experienced yesterday. This is possible because it is assumed that there are patterns in the world that can be relied upon and extrapolated from. In other words, if it has always happened one way, it is believed that it will continue to be that way.

> If every time you ate at a restaurant you had a nice experience, you conclude that you will have a nice experience the next time.

> If you always left for school 20 minutes before classes started and were never late, you judge that you can do the same today.

> If you have never missed when you shot the eight ball into the corner pocket while playing billiards, you bet that you won't miss this time either.

In general, it is rational to assume that we can make some predictions on the basis of our past experiences. For example, "Every zebra I've seen in the past has been striped; therefore, the next zebra I see will also be striped." Assuming the premise is true (that I have in fact seen a large number of zebras, and they've all been striped), this inductive argument is strong.

A person acts rationally when he or she acts upon reasonable beliefs that are based on satisfactory and sufficiently supportive premises, even if those beliefs turn out to be false. If you assume that tomorrow will be just like today or at least similar to today, then you can make plans for it. You believe the sun will rise tomorrow because it has done so every morning that you or anyone else has been on the planet. All things considered, it is rational to make life plans on the assumption that you will be alive in 10 years, next year, tomorrow, and 10 minutes from now, but these predictions can still turn out false!

Nevertheless, you cannot *prove* what will happen in the future on the basis of the past. The sun may have risen for as long as anyone can remember, but you can't prove it will rise tomorrow. This is because to "prove" is to achieve the kind of certainty that is only possible in a deductive argument. The so-called **problem of induction** is that you can't be sure that what has happened in the past will continue on in the future or that what has caused something to happen previously will continue to do so in the future. Why? Because it hasn't happened yet, so you can't verify it! You can't even base the future success of induction on the

Problem of Induction: A problem with inductive reasoning about future events. The problem is that we can in general never be certain that future events will resemble past events, so no matter how many observations we've made about the past, we can't be certain that those observations will help us to accurately predict the future. Despite this problem, reasoning on the basis of strong inductive arguments is rational.

successfulness of induction in the past because, again, those past events don't prove anything about the future.

Still, you rightfully live every moment of your life as if you can predict the future on the basis of the past; in fact, you have to. Yes, it is true that one day the sun might not rise, but all things considered, it is probably not going to happen tomorrow. So you better get that homework done, because your instructor is not going to like the excuse that you weren't sure whether morning would ever come.

Sample Size and Representation

Inductive arguments often involve statistical generalizations, such as "Eight out of 10 vampires prefer type O negative blood" or "Fifty-eight per cent of people don't like to be categorized." When generalizing about a group it is often imprac-

Sample: A subset selection of a population. Samples are used for inductive generalizations.

tical to ask or examine every member of the group, so a small **sample** is examined and then this information is extrapolated to the larger group. You don't examine every smoker to conclude that smoking is a health hazard. You don't need to ask every soda drinker in order to conclude that eight out of 10 people prefer one particular brand over the competition—but you'd better ask more than just 10! You shouldn't conclude, for example, that "there are no good people in Ontario" on the basis of two bad experiences.

Target Population: All individuals within the population that is being considered. For example, if you are attempting to determine the favourite book of Canadian school children, the target population is Canadian school children.

You may wish to ask 1,000 Canadians for whom they are going to vote in the next federal election and draw a conclusion about all Canadians on that basis. If 600 of the 1,000 people asked are going to vote for the Conservatives, then you might reasonably conclude that approximately 60 per cent of all Canadians are going to vote for the Conservatives. (This sample size is just for sake of argument and does not reflect the actual numbers used by professional pollsters.)

The smaller the sample, the more qualified your conclusion must be. This is why, when you hear poll results, they will stipulate a degree of accuracy that is plus or minus a certain percentage (e.g., "Sixty per cent of Canadians will vote

Representative Sample: A sample that has the same distribution of all relevant characteristics as the whole population being considered.

Conservative plus or minus 3 per cent," so the actual percentage predicted is between 57 and 63 per cent). Moreover, scope can come into play depending upon your sample size. Based upon your findings, it may be that only a few Canadians will vote Conservative—or some will, or many, or most.

Perhaps even more important than sample size is proper representation. You must have an accurate representation of the **target population** so that your sample reflects any variety that exists within it. That is, if you are talking about students, then you should be polling a **representative sample** of students. This seems pretty straightforward, but it means that you should not seek out only

Random Sample: A sample in which every member of the represented population has an equal prospect of being included.

business students, or first-year students, or just males with dark hair if you wish to draw a satisfactory generalization about all students. Once you have determined the target population, you should seek a **random sample** by ensuring that every member of the target population has an equal prospect of being included. Consider the following:

After discovering that 70 per cent of people at the $1,000-a-plate fundraiser own expensive imported cars, you conclude that 70 per cent of all citizens own expensive imports.

Is this inductively strong? No. The sample is not representative since the sample group is probably more wealthy than most other citizens and would thus have a greater likelihood of owning a more expensive car.

POLLING GUIDELINES

1. Determine what the sample and target population are. Do they match?
2. Is the sample size small? This may be acceptable if the population is itself small or uniform, but in general a larger sample is best.
3. The greater the variety of the target population, the larger the sample size required.
4. How has the sample been selected? Is it random?

Statistical Accuracy

One of the things that distinguishes Canada from its neighbour to the south is its national health care system. When asked in opinion polls, the vast majority of Canadians prefer our system of universal coverage over the US individual payer model. What this pool result actually means however can be affected by how the original question was phrased and which sorts of people were asked. Thus, one needs to be careful and examine how surveys and their statistical results are put together and presented. For example, if one was asked "Do you prefer the health care system of Canada?," one might say, "Yes. If I had to choose between the Canadian health care system and say, having a bowling ball dropped on my foot, I would choose the former." In other words, the question—as posed—is vague since a person would then ask "preferable to what?"

If one was asked "Do you like your health care?," one might answer differently than if asked, "Do you like the Canadian health care system?" because the former is about the person's direct experiences within the system, whereas the latter is a general question about the social institution. Furthermore, different people might interpret the questions "Do you like the Canadian health care system?" and "Do you prefer the Canadian health care system over the US pay-as-you-go system?" differently. One respondent might answer within the context of how well the system actually works, while another might answer the question as if it were about the ideals of what a health care system should look like.

Even if the question is phrased appropriately, one has to be concerned over whether the poll was truly random and representative of Canadians. Who did they ask? Are they asking young adults as well as older ones since these groups will have different health care issues? Are people from every province being asked, as well as those in large cities where there are large hospitals and rural towns where even access to a family doctor may be difficult? Did they only ask people who were waiting in overflowing emergency rooms or did they only approach those whose experiences were much better? Did they ask the wealthy and the poor and some people in-between? How many people did they ask? 10? 10,000?

You need to put on your critical thinking toque when you hear people using statistics.

Here is a lighter example. Consider an advertisement that tells you "Three out of four dentists recommend our gum." Three out of four dentists equals 75 per cent—but 75 per cent of what? All dentists? Well, it doesn't say that. Maybe they only asked four dentists in total. Or maybe they asked four dentists who work for the gum company. Perhaps they first asked four independent dentists and only one of them recommended the product. In that case, since the company could never sell an item by stating "Hey, one dentist liked it!," they might have found another four dentists and used only the new result.

Now suppose they asked four dentists and all four liked the product. This would be perfect, wouldn't it? Actually no, because in the minds of the consumer "four out of four" means 100 per cent and thus translates into "Every dentist recommends our gum." As it is not the case that the company actually asked every practising dentist, it would be easy for the consumer to refute this claim, since only one dentist would have to not recommend the gum.

What about two dentists out of four recommending the gum? Are these odds good enough for an advertisement? Two out of four gives you a 50 per cent chance that a specific dentist likes it. If that were the case, then you might as well toss a coin and choose whether to buy the product or not. So three out of four dentists is a good result to use. It isn't overly confident, but it is a safe number. It is safe because if you asked your dentist if she recommended the product, and she said, "No," you could conclude that she was in the 25 per cent group.

Consider the advertising claim that "More people prefer brand X cola than brand Y." How many more people? A vast majority or just one teenager who happened to say, "Eh, I guess X is a little bit better"? Again, how many people were asked is one question, but an equally important question is who was asked. Did they randomly select people of all ages from all walks of life and from all parts of the country?

Imagine that the label or container design of the cola is "modern" and aimed towards a younger consumer. Did the people who chose this product choose it for its taste or how it looked? Did they choose it because they had heard it advertised a million times more than some other cola or because they knew all their friends liked it and they didn't want to seem different? How were they given the choice? Did the company representative say, "Would you like to try a taste test? You look like the kind of person who really knows what they want. I bet you have a great sense of taste to go along with your fine sense of style. Here, first try our brand, which sexy millionaires sip at really cool parties; now try the competitor's brand—you know, the brand that heroin addicts like to drink." Surely, in that case, you wouldn't want to say the competitor's product is better even if you thought it was!

Statistics don't lie, but the people who use them might. Okay, that's probably too harsh. Let's say instead that sometimes the people who use statistics may not have thought carefully about the validity of their research or may not be giving you enough information to properly analyze their numbers. So watch out for the sample size and see whether the selection of individuals is truly random or whether it overrepresents some individuals and underrepresents others. When you hear numbers and percentages thrown around, ask yourself: What do they really reveal?

5.6 Evaluating Arguments from Analogy

Using an argument from analogy involves comparing cases and subsequently drawing a conclusion based upon the strength of the similarities between those cases. In other words, you note that Case A has essential features 1, 2, and 3, and that these lead it to have feature 4. Case B has features 1, 2, and 3 as well, so by analogy you conclude it too will have feature 4. The attraction of these types of arguments is that they are easy to construct and they appeal to consistency, which is an inherent feature of rational thought. To reason consistently is to treat like cases alike. So if A is the same as B and A leads to C, then B should lead to C as well. If Jane got 93 per cent on the test and John got 93 per cent on the test, then whatever letter grade Jane gets, John should get the same.

Analogies can be extremely useful for helping people to grasp ideas that they might not otherwise have understood or accepted. For example, suppose Sheila tells you she has an Akita. You say, "What is that?" She replies, "It's a dog. It looks sort of like an Alaskan husky. You know, the kind that pulls sleds up North." Since you're probably already familiar with husky-type dogs, comparing her dog to a husky gives you a rough idea about the kind of dog she owns. It's important to keep in mind that analogies used in this way are sometimes explanations, not arguments.

When you are arguing, you can use analogies effectively by getting your opponents to agree with one claim and then showing them how that particular claim is similar to another. For example, suppose you're playing on a trivia quiz team. You catch your opponents sharing answers with another team, but they see nothing wrong with this. So you decide to use an analogy. You first get them to agree that if a student shared his or her answers with a fellow classmate during an exam, this would be morally wrong. You then draw the comparison between playing a game, where there are cash prizes for having right answers, and writing an exam, where good grades are rewarding in other ways. The relevant similarity is that in both cases something significant is at stake. Finally, you conclude that if it is wrong of the student to share his or her answers, then it would be wrong for members on the trivia quiz team to share theirs.

You must be careful when making and evaluating arguments that use analogies, since there are both similarities and dissimilarities between any two items. Vodka and water are alike in that they are both clear liquids, but you don't want to drink a large glass of vodka before you go out for a Sunday drive. Zombies and vampires are both undead creatures, but one can survive in sunlight and the other one cannot.

Once you've determined what the similarities are, you'll need to determine whether they are relevant to the argument. The fact that two people writing an exam are both named Anna does not mean that the instructor should give them the same grade. Sure, they both have the same name, but that is irrelevant to what they deserve on the exam. Likewise, if there were two students with different names, say, Conrad and Charlotte, and they both scored 90 out of 100 on the exam, the dissimilarity in their names is irrelevant to the letter grade they should receive. That they received the same score *is* relevant.

Traditionally, arguments from analogy are assessed as **strong**, **weak**, or **faulty**. A *strong* argument from analogy will have *relevant similarities* between the primary subject and analogue and either no differences or differences that are irrelevant. A *weak* argument from analogy will have few, if any, relevant similarities but will contain *relevant differences*. In a *faulty* argument from analogy, there is nothing relevant in common between the primary subject and analogue.

Here is a strong argument from analogy:

P1) Patient A had the following symptoms: runny nose, fever, and a headache; we determined that A had a cold.

P2) Patient B has the same symptoms as A.

C3) Therefore, B probably has a cold.

Here is a weak argument from analogy:

P1) Patient A didn't feel well last week.

P2) Patient B doesn't feel well now.

C3) Therefore, B probably has the same illness as A.

Here is a faulty argument from analogy:

P1) Patient A didn't feel well last week.

P2) Patient B feels fine.

C3) Therefore, B probably has the same illness as A.

When determining which similarities and differences are relevant, you should pay careful attention to the context of the argument. Suppose you see a restaurant with a large lineup out front; you might conclude that, because other restaurants

Strong Argument from Analogy: An argument from analogy in which the primary subject and the analogue case have relevant similarities and either no differences or only irrelevant differences.

Weak Argument from Analogy: An argument from analogy in which the primary subject and the analogue case have few relevant similarities or have relevant dissimilarities.

Faulty Analogy: An argument from analogy in which the primary subject and the analogue case have no similarities or only irrelevant similarities.

with large lineups have served you delicious food (presumably their popularity is a sign of quality), *this* restaurant is also likely to have delicious food. But now suppose that it's the only restaurant in a busy airport; the large lineup, because it's not in this case an indicator of popularity, is no longer a relevant similarity, and so the argument by analogy becomes weak.

Consider the following argument from analogy:

> Harold robbed a grocery store and Julie robbed a gas station. Both of them had a weapon. Therefore, whatever punishment Harold gets, Julie should get as well.

In this example, you should note that both individuals committed the same crime under apparently similar circumstances. In order to be consistent, we should say that if two people do the same crime, they should do the same time. In this example, there is no mention of any *relevant* differences. True, they robbed different types of businesses (one a grocery store, the other a gas station), and they have different names and genders, but these differences seem irrelevant. Relevant differences would include such things as whether anyone was hurt, whether one used a gun as a weapon and the other used a baseball bat, whether one confessed and the other did not, whether it was the first crime for one and the tenth for the other, etc. Each of these would play a crucial role in determining the appropriate sentences after the robbers are found guilty and whether justice would be served if they received the same punishments.

Consider the situation where Conrad received 90 per cent on his exam, as did Charlotte. Their professor gave Charlotte an A but failed Conrad.

Did the professor reason poorly? It would seem so, given the relevant similarities. However, if you added to this case that Conrad cheated by copying Charlotte's answers, and the professor knew this, you can see that the professor's decision may have been correct. The relevant difference between the two cases (that one cheated and the other didn't) outweighs the seemingly relevant similarity (that the students received the same numerical score), and so the analogy is weak.

Some analogies may appear to cite relevant similarities but in fact depend on ambiguities or misleading wording. The following, for example, is a faulty analogy:

> When steam builds up in a covered pot of boiling water, the lid will come off.
> Anger in people can build up like steam in a pot.
> Therefore, to avoid "losing your lid," you should vent your anger.

The primary subject is the buildup of anger in people. This is being compared to a pot of boiling water releasing steam. Although we can speak of "letting off steam," "losing your lid," and "venting" in both cases, the language is only metaphorical when we're talking about people. Indeed, it is not always the case that people should express (or "vent") their anger, because in some situations it would be inappropriate (e.g., a student swearing at a professor because she has been falsely accused of cheating) and perhaps even dangerous (e.g., a commercial pilot who discovers that her husband is cheating on her should not let off steam while in the air). The "steam argument" relies on a faulty analogy because it attempts to compare two cases that have no relevant similarities.

There are two types of arguments from analogy: *a priori* **analogies** and **inductive analogies**. With *a priori* analogies, the arguer is drawing a comparison in which the analogue may be fictitious or hypothetical—whether or not the analogue is real has no effect upon the logical force of the argument.

> Robin Hood stole from the rich to give to the poor, and he was a hero. So, if I can get money out of the hands of the wealthy and give it to those who need it most, even by cheating and lying, I'll be a hero too.

Whether or not Robin Hood really existed has no bearing on the strength of this argument. The accuracy of the description of the analogue case is unimportant. But the accuracy of the primary subject's description is important even in an *a priori* analogy. Consider the following example:

> Robin Hood stole from the rich to give to the poor, and he was a hero. Like Robin Hood, Elvis Presley stole from the rich to give to the poor. Therefore, Elvis Presley is also a hero.

This analogy fails because the primary subject—in this case, Elvis Presley—didn't steal from the rich to give to the poor. Even though, for the purposes of this argument, it doesn't matter whether Robin Hood really existed, it *does* matter whether the claims made about Elvis are true.

With inductive analogies, the analogue must be a real case, and the features of the case are crucial. Inductive analogies are often used for making predictions. Consider:

> So far, all the animal subjects that our lab has tested have been cured using this drug. We now know that the drug is effective and is safe for humans.

With this example, it is important that the details of the tests are accurately presented and that the tests do actually reveal what is claimed.

Arguments from Analogy and the S-Test

When you apply the S-Test to arguments from analogy, each step is a little bit different from other applications of the S-Test.

The standards for satisfactoriness vary depending on what kind of analogy you're considering. In an *a priori* analogy, the description of the analogue is always satisfactory, since the argument can still work even if the analogue is completely made-up—but it's still possible for the description of the primary subject to be unsatisfactory. An inductive analogy, on the other hand, only passes the first step of the S-Test if all the premises satisfy the usual standards for satisfactoriness.

The standard for sufficient support is that there must be (a) relevant similarities between the analogue and the primary subject and (b) few relevant differences. To see if there is support, look for similarities between the analogue and the primary subject. For the argument to pass this step of the test, there must be similarities—and at least some of those similarities must be relevant to the conclusion.

To evaluate sufficiency of support, consider the differences between the primary subject and the analogue. If these differences are irrelevant to the comparison being made in the argument, ignore them and accept the argument. (For example, if you were inferring a drug's effectiveness for one patient on the basis of its effectiveness for another, differences such as the patients' names would count as irrelevant.) Relevant differences, however, reduce the strength of the argument. (For example, if the first patient was of a different gender, age, weight, and species, this would greatly reduce the strength of the argument.) Support is sufficient only if there aren't too many relevant differences between the analogue and the primary subject.

When evaluating an argument from analogy, apply the S-Test as follows:

1. *Satisfactoriness*: In the case of an inductive analogy, are all the premises factually accurate? In the case of an *a priori* analogy, you don't need to evaluate the description of the analogue for satisfactoriness, but you may still need to evaluate the description of the primary subject. If the argument fails this step of the test, it is a bad argument.

2. *Support*: Determine which features of the analogue are relevant to the conclusion. Given the context, are there relevant similarities between these features and those of the primary subject? If there are no similarities or if there are only irrelevant similarities, then the argument fails this step of the test and is a faulty analogy.

3. *Sufficient Support*: How many relevant similarities and differences are there? The number of relevant similarities and differences will affect the analogy's strength; if there are many relevant similarities and few relevant differences, then the analogy is strong. The weighting of similarities and differences is highly contextual; sometimes a single relevant difference is enough to make an analogy weak, while in other cases an analogy may be strong despite one or two relevant differences. For this reason, arguments from analogy are often inductive in that they establish their conclusions to a certain degree of probability, not with certainty.

5.7 Chapter Exercises

Exercise 5.1

TRUE/FALSE QUESTIONS

1. If a deductive argument is valid, then it must be sound. True or False?
2. If a deductive argument is sound, then it must be valid. True or False?
3. A strong analogy has no dissimilarities between the cases that are being compared. True or False?
4. Inductive arguments often forecast how the future may be on the basis of events in the past. True or False?
5. Strong inductive arguments can sometimes lead to false conclusions. True or False?

Exercise 5.2

Read each of the following passages and determine whether it is a deductive argument, an inductive argument, or an argument from analogy. Don't try to figure out if they are good arguments or bad, just examine their structure.

1. Every day I've worked here, my boss has ordered the same thing for lunch. He calls me to place the order for him. Let's see, it's almost noon now. So he'll be asking me to place an order for his usual lunch.
2. Jazz is better than rock music because jazz is made up of complex arrangements like classical music. Classical music has been around for centuries and has withstood the passage of time. I suspect jazz and not rock will do the same.
3. I have owned three smartphones and none of them had long-lasting batteries. This new one cost me a lot more, thus I bet it will have a longer-lasting battery for sure.
4. The weather along the east coast has been much more dramatic these past years. Every year there have been more storms than the year before and the storms lately have been stronger than ever. We're about to enter hurricane season, therefore those on the east coast should expect some significant weather events over and above what they have experienced in the last few years.
5. I have DNA. You have DNA. Bats have DNA. Therefore, all living things have DNA.
6. All living things have DNA. I am a living thing. Therefore, I have DNA.
7. As far as I can tell based on your dumb actions, your brain is about the size of a dinosaur's. The dinosaurs didn't manage to live that long, so I think you better smarten up.
8. I have a bag of different coloured marbles. Ten are black and 2 are red. With my eyes closed, I just removed a red marble from the bag, so the next one I remove will probably be black.

9. When you steal something from a store, you are shoplifting. When you steal, you are harming the owners by not compensating them for the product you have taken. If you're like me, you wouldn't steal from a store even if the owners weren't looking and there was no way for them to find you afterwards, because it's immoral. When you share or download music files from peer to peer websites without permission of the original artist (or the recording company), you are causing harm. Therefore, if shoplifting is immoral, so is downloading files like this.

10. Everyone who had an income last year must submit a tax return to the Canada Revenue Agency. You worked part time last fall, so you need to do your taxes.

Exercise 5.3

Consider the following three arguments. One is deductive, one is inductive, and one is an argument from analogy. Which is which?

1. I have red hair. You have red hair. She has red hair. Therefore, everyone has red hair.
2. Every person has red hair. I am a person. So I have red hair.
3. I am a person and you are a person. I have red hair, thus you have red hair too.

Exercise 5.4

For each of the following claims, create a deductive argument, an inductive argument, and an argument from analogy. The claims can be used as premises, conclusions, or parts of premises. Your arguments do not have to be successful.

1. There is life on other planets.
2. People like roses.
3. Cell phones are very handy these days.
4. It is important to get plenty of rest when at university.
5. Politicians are public servants.

Exercise 5.5

Create a conclusion (that starts with 'It is') by randomly selecting a term from each column, a to d. Then randomly pick a category from column e and supply premises to create an argument of that category in support of your conclusion. If you are asked to create a weak argument, don't just make up something silly. Instead, try to come up with something that someone might actually state. Present your argument to a colleague to discuss. Try to do this a few times since practice is important and because there are hundreds of possible combinations available for you to play with!

STATEMENT GENERATOR: MORAL ISSUES CONCLUSIONS

		a	b		c	d	e
1	It is	Always	Obligatory	for	Adults	To read or watch something offensive from the Internet.	Inductive Argument
2		Usually	Right		Children	To kill a robber in the act of committing the crime.	Argument from Analogy
3		Sometimes	Permissible		Community members	To keep money found in a wallet on the street.	Valid Deductive Argument
4		Hardly ever	Wrong		Family members	To solicit prostitutes.	Invalid Deductive Argument
5		Never	Prohibited		Friends	To steal if it will keep them from starving.	

Now try the same exercise with some arguments that might come up in a workplace:

STATEMENT GENERATOR: BUSINESS ISSUES CONCLUSIONS

		a	b		c	d	e
1	It is	Always	Obligatory	for	CEOs	To take inexpensive office supplies home.	Inductive Argument
2		Usually	Right		Bosses	To check personal email while at work.	Argument from Analogy
3		Sometimes	Permissible		Employees	To accept gifts from potential clients.	Valid Deductive Argument
4		Hardly ever	Wrong		Family members	To bribe officials if that is standard business practice in their country.	Invalid Deductive Argument
5		Never	Prohibited		Friends	To talk to the competition about a new job.	

Exercise 5.6

Identify whether each of the following is a deductive argument, an inductive argument, or an argument by analogy. Then, taking its argument type into account, use the S-Test to determine whether it is sound/unsound, valid/invalid, strong/weak, or strong/weak/faulty.

1. P1) Everything that grows naturally is safe to eat.

    P2) Deadly nightshade grows naturally.

    C3) Therefore, deadly nightshade is safe to eat.

2. P1) I was too afraid to sleep after I read Thomas Harris's horror novel
    The Silence of the Lambs.

    P2) The movie *The Silence of the Lambs* is based on the book and has a
    similar plot.

    C3) Therefore, if I watch the movie *The Silence of the Lambs* tonight,
    I'll probably be too afraid to sleep afterward.

3. P1) I asked every member of the Toronto Symphony Orchestra whether they
    liked Beethoven, and 90 per cent of the people I surveyed said they did.

    C2) Therefore, most people in Canada like Beethoven.

4. P1) My friend Carrie is from the Maritimes, her name starts with C, and she
    scored 95 per cent on her French test.

    P2) My friend Candice is also from the Maritimes, and her name also starts
    with C.

    C3) Therefore, Candice probably also scored 95 per cent on her French test.

5. P1) This cactus is either dead or alive.

    P2) This cactus is not dead.

    C3) Therefore, this cactus is alive.

5.8 Postscript

Three common argument types are discussed in this chapter: deductive, inductive, and arguments from analogy. Deductive arguments aim for certainty while the other two aim for strength.

In this and the previous chapter, we discussed the use of the S-test for evaluating arguments. While all arguments can be evaluated using the S-Test, each argument type also has some unique features that are important to keep in mind. For example, deductive arguments can be tested for validity: if the premises of a deductive argument don't (if true) *guarantee* the truth of the argument's conclusion, then the argument is invalid. This means that the premises of deductive arguments require a greater degree of sufficiency than do the premises of an inductive argument or an argument by analogy.

And, while we must always test whether the premises of inductive and deductive arguments are satisfactory, the same is not always true of arguments by analogy. An *a priori* argument by analogy can use a fictional or false analogue case to make a strong argument about a real case. So, while the S-Test offers an effective general strategy for evaluating arguments, we must keep in mind the exceptions that come up with particular argument types.

CHAPTER 6
Fallacies

Fallacies are intentional or unintentional errors in reasoning. They are often psychologically persuasive since they mimic successful approaches to argumentation and thus can fool people who are inexperienced in critical thinking. Sometimes people commit fallacies because they are not good arguers, but other times people commit fallacies deliberately, so as to persuade others to accept a conclusion.

Philosophers have identified a great many fallacies, and you're likely already aware of some of them. In this chapter we'll look at some of the more common fallacies, which any good critical thinker should learn to recognize.

Fallacy: An intentional or unintentional error in reasoning.

6.1 List of Fallacies

We can divide fallacies up roughly according to three criteria of the S-Test. Some fallacies usually affect the satisfactoriness of an argument's premises, while others typically undermine the support that those premises grant to the conclusion or the sufficiency of that support. As you work through the steps of the S-Test, it would be wise to keep in mind the fallacies most often associated with each step.

Fallacies Associated with Satisfactoriness

Amphiboly: In this fallacy, the structure of a sentence allows two different interpretations.

The professor said Sarah is smart, but she's not wise.

Problem: Amphibolies can create situations in which people interpret the same claim differently. Is the statement above saying (a) "The professor said Sarah is smart but unwise," or (b) "The unwise professor said Sarah is smart?" This fallacy may undermine the satisfactoriness of an argument's premises, or it may make the connection between the premises and the conclusion unclear.

Begging the Question: In this fallacy, the truth of the conclusion is already assumed in the premises.

Abortion is murder. So abortion is wrong.

Problem: Here, the conclusion simply paraphrases the premise, since murder is, by definition, wrong. In order to consider the premise of this argument satisfactory, therefore, one has to have already accepted its conclusion. The argument is thus unpersuasive to any person who doesn't already agree with the arguer.

Equivocation: Fallacy in which the same term is used with two different meanings, but the argument treats both meanings as if they were the same.

The jury found me innocent. Therefore, as an innocent man, I did nothing wrong.

Problem: Arguments can be fallacious if they use the same words without proper continuity of meaning. Here, the word "innocence" has two different meanings. The first is a legal meaning: if he is legally innocent, then he wasn't convicted, perhaps only because there wasn't enough evidence. The second meaning is moral: if he is morally innocent, then he did nothing wrong. But he could be legally innocent and not morally innocent, so the conclusion does not follow from the premise. In this case, either the premise is unsatisfactory (if it is meant to assert that the man is morally innocent), or it fails to support the conclusion (if it only asserts the man's legal innocence).

False Dilemma: In a false dilemma, only two choices are given when in fact there are more options.

Either you are with us or you are against us.

Problem: In most situations, there are more than two options available. In this case, for example, you might be disinterested and not care one way or the other. Or you might agree to some extent but have some reservations.

Improper Appeal to Authority: In this fallacy, the authority that provides support for the conclusion is either not an expert in the relevant area, or is not honest and reliable, or is not in agreement with other experts in this area, or the area is not something that one can be an authority about.

The physician I go to is really smart. I think her views on the morality of plastic surgery should be listened to.

Problem: The fact that a person is an authority in one area does not make that individual an authority in others. A physician's possession of medical knowledge does not make him or her a moral expert. If an authority is not a credible source of information in general, then his or her claims are likely unsatisfactory. If, on the other hand, an authority is honest and reliable but not an expert in a relevant area, his or her claims may be satisfactory but not supportive of the argument's conclusion.

Inconsistency: An argument in which contrary or contradictory statements are asserted to be true at the same time.

Hey, let's all go downhill skiing this weekend. I know you hate skiing and my wife doesn't like to go out in the cold, but it will be fun for us all!

Problem: Given that the arguer has suggested that some people would not enjoy skiing, it is inconsistent to also say it would be fun for everyone. The two statements cannot both be true at the same time, so at least one of this argument's premises must be false.

Straw Person Argument: In a straw person argument, the arguer reconstructs an opponent's argument as something weaker than it actually is, then attacks that weaker version of the argument.

Richard: Studies have shown that the teaching of abstinence is the most effective way to reduce rates of teenage pregnancy. This should be the standard practice in our schools, not contraceptive education.

Suzette: I want our children to learn about safe sex practices; you want them to believe that sex is a sin!

Problem: This type of fallacy (which used to be called a "straw man argument") gets its name from the idea that you can knock down a straw figure more easily than a real person; similarly, it is easier to knock down an artificial argument than a real one. In this example, the initial argument says nothing about sin, but rather appeals to evidence. A legitimate objection would question the evidence itself or the connection between the evidence and the conclusion; instead, the response here misrepresents the argument so as to make it less convincing.

This fallacy is common in political debates. It also happens accidentally when one arguer does not quite understand what another arguer is claiming; this is why it is important that you ensure that you understand another person's views before expressing your disagreement.

Fallacies Associated with Support

Abusive Ad Hominem: *Ad hominem* is a Latin phrase meaning "to the person." In an abusive ad hominem fallacy, an individual's character is attacked, rather than his or her arguments.

> Elsa: It seems to me that suffering is often caused by a lack of social engagement;
> so if we wish to eliminate suffering, we should encourage socializing.
> Dave: What do you know about suffering? Look at you, you're beautiful!

Problem: That a person is young, old, rich, poor, smart, foolish, wise, or immature is usually irrelevant to the merits or demerits of his or her argument.

Ad Hominem Tu Quoque: In Latin, *tu quoque* means "you too!" In a tu quoque fallacy, an argument is rejected because the arguer does not act in accordance with his or her own conclusion.

> Why should I listen to your lessons about abstaining from smoking? You started
> smoking when you were 12!

Problem: That the person doesn't listen to his or her own argument doesn't entail that it's a bad argument. Here, the smoker may be offering a good argument against smoking, even if he or she nonetheless smokes.

Affirming the Consequent: This argument takes the form:

> If A, then B
> B
> _____
> Therefore, A.

This argument form is always invalid.

> If it is raining out, then the streets are wet. The streets are wet. Therefore, it is
> raining out.

Problem: This argument assumes that since B (the "consequent") is true, A (the "antecedent") must also be true. But the original statement ("If A, then B") only tells us what we can know if A is true; it doesn't tell us what we can know if B is true. In this case, there could be other reasons why the streets are wet. For example, it could be snowing or the street cleaners could be out.

Appeal to Force: This is an attempt to persuade through threat of harm.

> I think you'll agree that the terms of this new contract are fair; otherwise you may
> find yourself looking for work elsewhere in these difficult economic times.

Problem: Threats to a person's economic, physical, or psychological well-being can be quite intimidating, but are irrelevant to whether the claims made by the arguer are true.

Appeal to Pity: This is an attempt to persuade on grounds of compassion when compassion is not relevant to the argument.

> I can't be guilty of robbery, your Honour! I have a family that needs me out of prison so I can work and put food on the table.

Problem: On its own, pity is not a legitimate reason to accept an argument. In this case, the nature of the unfortunate situation is irrelevant to the satisfactoriness of the claim. Whether or not the judge feels sorry for the accused doesn't have any bearing on whether or not the accused committed the crime. Compassion may, however, be relevant in some cases; here, it may be relevant to the judge's decision regarding a proper sentence.

Appeal to Popularity: In an appeal to popularity, a claim is argued to be true on the grounds that it is widely believed to be true.

> There has to be life after death. Millions of people from cultures across the world believe in an afterlife!

Problem: While the popularity of a belief might be justified if the belief is true, that people believe something doesn't make the belief true. Popular views are not necessarily the correct ones. At one time most people believed the sun revolved around the earth, but they were simply incorrect.

Appeal to Tradition: An assertion that because something has always been done a certain way, that way is correct.

> I come from a family with a long history of trapping animals for fur. I don't see anything wrong with it.

Problem: The long-term practices of this person's family are no more immune to criticism than are practices that have only been taken up recently.

Circumstantial Ad Hominem: In a circumstantial ad hominem fallacy, an argument is rejected on the grounds that the arguer has some ulterior motive.

> You want to remove the gas tax just because you know that doing so will help you get re-elected.

Problem: An argument may still have merit regardless of whether the arguer has ulterior motives for presenting it.

Denying the Antecedent: This argument takes the form:

P1) If A, then B.

P2) Not A.

——————

C3) Therefore, Not B.

This argument form is always invalid.

> If this creature is a dog, then it is a mammal. It is not a dog. Therefore, it must not be a mammal.

Problem: The argument assumes that since A (the "antecedent") is false, B (the "consequent") must be false, too. But the original statement ("If A, then B") only tells us what we can know if A is *true*; it doesn't tell us what we can know if A is *false*. In this case, the fact that the creature is not a dog does not mean that it is not some other kind of mammal.

Guilt by Association: In this fallacy, a person's views are rejected because those views are associated with a group that is unpopular.

> Sure, Canada has socialized medicine, but so did the old Soviet Union.

Problem: A view may be correct, or an argument may be strong, even if it is associated with a disreputable group. In this example, the fact that the socialized medicine was practised in a society that is widely perceived as unjust does not itself show that socialized medicine is bad.

Red Herring: A red herring occurs when an arguer wanders from his or her argument to some other unrelated or tangential point, thereby distracting the audience.

> How can you accuse me of taking steroids to promote my career in baseball? I give money to charities. I volunteer at the local food bank. I regularly speak at schools about the benefits of giving back to the community!

Problem: The person uses irrelevant claims to digress or misdirect the audience. Here, the individual offers positive descriptions of his or her character to divert attention away from the accusation of taking banned substances.

Two Wrongs Make a Right: In this fallacy, a wrong action is defended on the basis that someone else did the same thing.

> But officer, everyone else was speeding too!

Problem: The fact that other people did something wrong and were not punished is irrelevant to whether the act itself is wrong. The fact that others were speeding means that other people were also doing something wrong, not that everyone was doing something right. If the police officer could have ticketed all the speeders, she probably would have done so.

Fallacies Associated with Sufficiency

Appeal to Ignorance: This is an argument in which, because something is not known to be true, it is assumed to be false; or, because it is not known to be false, it is assumed to be true.

> No one has proven that ghosts are a figment of our imaginations. And given that so many people have claimed to see them, they must be out there.

Problem: Not knowing that something is false is different from knowing that it is true. In this case, the person has drawn a strong conclusion when in fact all that may be drawn is a tentative and indeterminate conclusion (that we aren't certain that ghosts don't exist).

Composition Fallacy: Fallacy in which, because the parts of a whole have a certain property, it is assumed that the whole has that property.

> The National Hockey League selected the best players to be on the All-Star team. So if that team were to play against any regular team, it would easily win.

Problem: The fact that the parts of the whole are good does not entail that the whole itself will be good. Here, the All Star players might not work well as a team, since they have not had a great deal of time to get to know each other as teammates.

Division Fallacy: This is a fallacy in which, because the whole has a certain property, it is assumed that the parts have that property.

> Her team won the national baseball championship, so she must be a great player.

Problem: This fallacy occurs when one assumes that all parts of a whole must have the same qualities as the whole. Here, the team might have won in spite of the poor playing of the individual team member.

Faulty Analogy: In an argument by analogy, the two objects or events being compared have no relevant similarities or are relevantly dissimilar.

> You want the government to ban guns because guns can kill. Well, I can kill a man by shoving a pencil into his ear. Do you want the government to ban pencils too?

Problem: An argument from analogy depends on the existence of relevant similarities between the primary subject and the analogue case, as well as a lack of relevant dissimilarities. While you can kill someone with a pencil, the fact that killing is not its intended function or standard use is a relevant difference between pencils and guns.

Hasty Generalization: A hasty generalization is a faulty generalization based on a small or unrepresentative sample size.

> The television news reporter asked all the people waiting at the bus stop who they were going to vote for next week in the national election, and it looks like the New Democratic Party (NDP) will definitely win a majority of seats.

Problem: One cannot generalize from one or two instances. In this case, what if everyone waiting for the bus was going to vote NDP? Would this entail that the NDP would get 100 per cent of all the votes cast in the national election? Surely not; the sample is too small to represent the entire population. It's also insufficiently diverse, since the reporter only asked people who take the bus and were waiting at a particular stop at a particular time.

Post Hoc: A fallacy in which an arguer claims that since one event happened before another event, the first event must have caused the second.

> Ever since I patted that stray cat, I've not been feeling well. I must have picked up something from it.

Problem: That one event occurs before another does not mean that the first event was the cause of the second. The events might have occurred in this order accidentally, or they might share some other common cause. In this case, the person is looking for a connection between two events without considering whether there is another possible cause. It is, of course, possible that patting the stray cat caused the illness, but more evidence would be required to conclude that this is the most likely explanation—mere causal succession is not enough.

Slippery Slope: This is a fallacy in which a series of increasingly unacceptable consequences are said to follow from an original position that appears to be acceptable. From this, it is claimed that the original position is therefore unsatisfactory.

> If Customs Canada and the Canadian government start demanding that everyone have a passport, sooner or later, people will have to carry identification papers with them everywhere they go, be it Halifax or rural Manitoba. Anytime a person is stopped, he or she will be expected to show these papers. Do you want to live in a police state like that?

Problem: Usually you can find a point in the "slope" where there is a relevant distinction to be drawn and it is no longer obvious that the alleged consequences will follow. For example, in this case, passports might only be required for travel to foreign countries and not required to be carried at all times.

6.2 Fallacies in Advertising

One place you frequently encounter fallacies is in advertising. It is claimed that the number of commercial advertisements that an average Canadian is exposed to in the course of a normal day ranges from a few hundred to a few thousand. The whole advertising industry exists to try to persuade you to "buy into" its messages, and the goal of advertising is persuade you to buy things that you may or may not need. Sometimes, advertising is not rational at all—it targets our emotions or unconscious thoughts—but when it targets our reason, it tends to use a variety of badly formed arguments that provide plenty of examples of fallacious reasoning.

Here are some fictional slogans and advertisements that may remind you of some real ads that you have seen. The intention is not to point fingers at specific companies or products (which is why no real name brands are used). Rather, it is to present some of the more typical and egregious flaws in reasoning that are used to (try to) get you to reach the conclusion the advertiser wants you to reach. Read the following few examples and see if you can pick out the problems in each. Some exhibit the problems discussed in earlier chapters, such as vagueness, insufficiency of support, etc.

1. Now with less salt!

Less salt than what? The competitors? Less salt than a full salt-shaker? How much less salt? One gram per serving? One hundred grams? This description is clearly too vague. Here, numbers matter, since the amount of an ingredient can be quantified. Any reduction, no matter how small, counts as "less." Furthermore, just because the salt has been reduced does not entail that the product as a whole is healthy (or healthier than it was before).

2. Everyone agrees: it's the best-selling shampoo today.

This is an obvious appeal to popularity. The advertisement is trying to plant in your head that because something is a bestseller, it must also be good (if not the best). Think of a popular song or movie that you hate; that it was a hit doesn't mean it was good. Perhaps the song, or movie, or shampoo, were all bestsellers because they were promoted the most. Or perhaps the shampoo is a bestseller because it is the cheapest—which doesn't mean that it is bad, but it doesn't necessarily mean it is very good either.

3. If you want to protect your family, you need these winter tires.

This is a sneaky example of appeal to force. The advertisement is appealing (not so subtly) to the fear that a parent has about his or her family being harmed. The implication of this argument is that if you don't get these tires, your family is in danger. Though not issuing a direct threat, the advertiser is implying that physical harm is a likely consequence of not purchasing the product. This is a rather unpleasant but common technique: threatening others with a bad consequence if they don't do what they're told. Winter tires are certainly important for safety in some circumstances, but buying this particular brand of tires is not the only way to protect your family's safety, and the threatening implication is inappropriate.

4. Are you going to eat salad every night? Or do you want something that actually tastes good? Eat at Grease Burger to satisfy your taste buds.

This is a classic example of a false dilemma. Most people don't want to eat salad every night, and the suggestion of a delicious but unhealthy meal seems an appealing alternative. But of course there are many delicious yet healthy foods, and one need not choose one extreme or the other.

5. Made with pure fruit!

This is a tricky one, but it is also an example of vagueness. The implication is that the product contains nothing but fruit, although in fact many "pure fruit" products have only 10 per cent fruit, the rest being water and sugar.

6. Since I've been on this diet plan, I've lost over 20 kilos! The program works!

This is a hasty generalization. One person's success isn't enough evidence to conclude that the program works. The small print in advertisements like this one usually also states that "individual results may vary" and that the program only works "when combined with regular physical exercise." These two caveats are necessary because one could (and is intended to) otherwise infer that the diet alone is sufficient for dramatic results and that if one person had those results, everyone else who follows the program will too.

7. Not only is he a movie star, he is a milk drinker.

This is an improper appeal to authority. The advertisement is drawing a connection between a celebrity and his behaviour. It is not uncommon for people to assume that individuals who are good at one thing (or famous) must know more about lots of things, including things that are irrelevant to their field (or to their fame). Unless this movie star also has some special expertise in nutrition, the fact that he chooses to drink milk is irrelevant to the implied conclusion that drinking milk is a good thing.

8. She uses our makeup and the world agrees: she looks fabulous.

This is another example of a hasty generalization. The ad seems to imply that anyone would look fabulous if they used this brand of makeup, which is surely false. This kind of ad is typically accompanied by imagery of a professional model— someone whose appearance is certainly not an unbiased representation of the population!

9. We use only the finest of ingredients. And so, of course, our pizza is the best.

This is an example of the composition fallacy. That the parts of the pizza are the best does not mean that the pizza itself is the best. Many other factors are relevant: the types of ingredients, their proportions, cooking time, etc.

As you can see, there are many different types of fallacies. You will encounter fallacies everywhere—not just in advertisements but also in news reports, political discussions, and everyday conversations—so it's useful to be able to spot them. The best way to learn how to recognize these errors is by looking at example after example. As you do this, the patterns should start to become clear.

6.3 Chapter Exercises

Exercise 6.1

TRUE/FALSE QUESTIONS

1. Not all fallacies are errors in reasoning. True or False?
2. People who commit a fallacy are intentionally trying to exploit another's ignorance about a particular issue. True or False?
3. Trying to win an argument by insulting your opponent is fallacious. True or False?
4. Stirring up people's emotions at an important sporting event is always fallacious. True or False?
5. Presuming someone is rational before knowing for sure is an example of the fallacy of ignorance. True or False?

Exercise 6.2

Pick up the local paper or magazine and glance at the editorials and letters to the editor. Pay attention to advertisements on television. Listen to people on a call-in radio show. How long does it take you to find an example of someone using fallacious reasoning? List the fallacies you encounter.

Exercise 6.3

Match the passage with the appropriate fallacy. There is only one instance of each fallacy.

1. No one has disproven the existence of Ogopogo, so there must be some prehistoric creature living in the lake near Kelowna.
2. Many honest people claim to have had out-of-body experiences, so there is good reason to believe in life after death.
3. We have never had a referendum in Ontario before so I see no reason to change that now.

4. If I am injured when I wear a seatbelt, I will sue the province; let's see how much that will cost you, the taxpayer! Seatbelts should be optional.

5. Parents in emerging nations don't have the luxury of receiving a monthly allowance, so why should the Canadian government give childcare allowances to parents here, especially given that the government is running a deficit?

6. Mothers know best. That's why they serve our brand of rice dishes more than any other.

(A) Faulty Analogy

(B) Appeal to Popularity

(C) Appeal to Tradition

(D) Appeal to Ignorance

(E) Improper Appeal to Authority

(F) Appeal to Force

Exercise 6.4

Determine which fallacy is being committed in each passage.

1. I know she loves me because she told me so and you don't lie to someone you love.

2. But Mom! She hit me first!

3. We are more aware now of the problems of animal abuse, but there have always been dog fights, especially in the poorer parts of the country. It's hard for people to change the views they grew up with. So it wouldn't be fair to ban dog fights.

4. Ever since I moved into that old dorm on campus, I have been sneezing and coughing like never before. There must be mold or something in that place that is causing my allergies to flare up. I'm going to see about trying to move into a better place.

5. You could tell that the movie was great by the fact that it was sold out again.

6. Big business owners always complain about the GST and other high taxes. Here they go again! Of course they think we all pay too many taxes—they just want to increase their own profit and pretend they are fighting for the taxpayer.

7. When my esteemed opponent argues against the new provincial legislation, she only reveals her ignorance of how the world works. Maybe if she spent some time working with real people instead of living in the land of fairies and magic, she'd realize how silly her view is.

8. He's not a very good player, but he tries really hard and I'd hate to disappoint him, so I'd say he's earned a spot on the team.

9. I'd love to help you out and give you an extension on your essay assignment, given that you've broken your writing hand. But if people find out that you got extra time, then everyone will be demanding the same treatment for all sorts of outrageous reasons.

10. This new phone app tells me that you and I are not a good match, so I think it's best that we just end our date now.

Exercise 6.5

Some of the following passages contain fallacies, and some of them do not. Determine whether a fallacy is being committed in each passage—and if there is a fallacy, identify which one.

1. Since I'm your teacher and have the power to give you detention at any time, I think you'll agree with me that high school gym class is the most fun you've ever had.
2. You say you love only me, but that can't be true. Just yesterday you told me you loved ice cream!
3. Either this goldfish is alive or it is dead.
4. Don't believe the city planner when she says that we can't put in a bike lane on Main Street. She's just afraid that if we put in the bike lane, she'll lose her parking space next to City Hall!
5. If you love me, you'll come to my show. You're coming to my show. Therefore, you love me.
6. I shouldn't be removed from office just because I've engaged in a few criminal activities. Other politicians get away with such things all the time!
7. Astronomers have discovered a planet that is the same temperature as Earth, has the same atmosphere as Earth, and has liquid water. Because it's so similar to Earth, it's possible that this planet could support life.
8. I believe that everyone has the right to express their opinions. People who think otherwise shouldn't be allowed to say so!
9. You can't expect me to consider becoming a vegetarian. Hitler was a vegetarian!
10. If you legalize marijuana, more people will start using it. Soon, everyone will be using it. Then those people will start experimenting with harder drugs, and before you know it the government will be pressured to legalize drugs like heroin and cocaine.
11. If I don't catch that bus, I'll be late for my classes. Oh no, it's already pulling away! I guess I'll miss Psychology this morning.
12. Same-sex marriage is wrong because marriage is supposed to be between a man and a woman.
13. Justin Bieber has sold more than 15 million albums. He must be a great musician!
14. I asked everybody in my Ancient Greek Philosophy class whether they had read Plato and Aristotle, and all of them have. Plato and Aristotle must be the most widely read writers in the world!
15. There's so much we don't know about the human brain! That's why I think extra-sensory perception is real.

16. I really like the Beatles. Since Ringo Starr was one of the Beatles, I'll really like his solo album.

17. If I take the dog for a walk, I will go outside. I'm not taking the dog for a walk. Therefore, I'm not going outside.

18. Don't believe anything Nietzsche wrote in his philosophy books. He went crazy before he died, you know.

19. You've been disrespecting your parents ever since you started going to university. It must be because of something you're learning there!

20. The members of Parliament being investigated say the members of the investigation committee are honest and impartial, but they're liars.

21. It might be a good idea to send your mother a card for her birthday, because if you don't she'll be really upset.

22. According to the Intergovernmental Panel on Climate Change, an organization established by the United Nations, climate change is almost certainly caused by human activity and is likely to have serious consequences for humankind. For these reasons, it's important for governments to work together to stop climate change.

23. It wouldn't be fair for you to give me an F on this essay. I know it's not written in complete sentences, but if you fail me you'll crush my dream of becoming a philosophy professor!

24. Zoe: The military shouldn't execute suspected terrorists without a trial because the right to a fair trial is guaranteed by the Universal Declaration of Human Rights.
    Walter: My opponent doesn't want the government to punish terrorists for their crimes!

25. My opponent claims that abstinence education is the most effective way to prevent teenage pregnancy, but the studies he is using were conducted by the Canadian Pro-Abstinence Association. Unbiased studies show that abstinence education isn't nearly as effective as my opponent says it is.

26. In Western civilization, men have been the heads of their households for thousands of years. Clearly, that's the way families are supposed to be.

27. Drinking a glass of beer from this keg made me feel really good. Therefore, if I drink the whole keg, I will feel great!

28. Don't tell me the neighbours will complain about the noise if I don't shut down this party! Yesterday you were practising the drums at 3 a.m.!

29. If you don't believe in Heaven and Hell, you must think it doesn't matter whether or not people lead morally good lives.

30. Don't vote for my opponent! The last time he held public office, he was convicted of embezzling public funds.

31. If I don't walk the dog, the dog might chew up my shoes. I'm not going to walk the dog. Therefore, the dog might chew up my shoes.

32. I can't believe you're saying cigarettes cause cancer. Radiation causes cancer! Asbestos causes cancer! Besides, I think smoking makes you look cool.

33. Hitler was very charismatic and was popular when he was elected. US President Obama is also very charismatic and was popular when he was elected. Clearly, Obama is a Nazi!

34. Stanley is a great veterinarian. He told me that my skin condition doesn't look serious, so I don't think I'll bother going to my physician.

6.4 Postscript

In previous chapters, we examined the S-Test, which is a way of assessing whether an argument is strong; any argument that passes the S-Test is a good argument. Sometimes, however, it's easier to assess an argument by first looking for problems. Any argument that exhibits one or more of the fallacies discussed in this chapter is likely to be weak in some way—it might have an unsatisfactory premise (if it requires, for example, an improper appeal to authority), it might lack sufficient support for its conclusion (if it begs the question or includes a red herring), or it might miss its target altogether (if it's a straw person argument).

It is difficult to appreciate errors of reasoning by merely reading their definitions. Without seeing example after example, one cannot appreciate the over 200 fallacies that have been identified by philosophers. However, fortunately or unfortunately, many people are poor arguers, so you will come across fallacies all the time (whether or not you notice them).

One minor point that should be mentioned is that there is some disagreement about what the best names are for various fallacies, so you may encounter different names than the ones given in this chapter. A good descriptive name helps a person understand what error is being made. For example, the term "hasty generalization" indicates exactly what the problem is whereas "straw person argument" is a more poetic name, but it is helpful nonetheless.

PART II

THE SCIENCE OF CRITICAL THINKING

PART II   THE SCIENCE
            OF CRITICAL
            THINKING

CHAPTER 7
Categorical Logic

At this point in the text you will notice a dramatic shift away from the "art" of critical thinking to the "science." You may have found the guidelines concerning the S-Test and the analysis of fallacies challenging because they require skills of interpretation and analysis that can only be developed through experience. With some deductive arguments, however, we can be more methodical in our analyses of support and sufficiency. In these last two chapters, we'll examine precise rules of logic that can help to eliminate some of the interpretive aspects of deductive reasoning.

It's important to remember, though, that these rules of logic do not apply to inductive reasoning or reasoning from analogy, nor do they work with all forms of deductive argument; in those cases, you must rely on the lessons discussed in earlier chapters. The rules of logic cannot tell you whether a given premise is satisfactory either. They are used strictly for determining whether a deductive argument's premises are sufficiently supportive. In this chapter, we'll examine categorical logic. First, we'll consider how to understand and manipulate individual categorical statements, and then we'll look at categorical syllogisms—arguments made up of categorical statements.

7.1 Categorical Logic and Categorical Statements

Categorical Logic: A subfield of formal logic that looks at the relationships between categories or groups.

Category: A group or collection of things.

Categorical Statement: A claim about whether the members of one category are, are not, or may be members of another category.

Subject Category: The group that a categorical statement says something about (e.g., in "All ants are insects," the subject category is "ants").

Predicate Category: The group that is related to the subject category in a categorical statement (e.g., in "All ants are insects," the predicate category is "insects").

A Statement: A categorical statement of the form "All S are P." This states that all members of S are members of P. Also called a "universal affirmative."

Developed by Aristotle, **categorical logic** deals with the relationships between real or abstract groups. Everything in the universe can be sorted into groups or **categories**: trees, dogs, rocks, rocks weighing over 10 kilograms, etc. Groups often overlap, as some members of one group may also belong to another group. Thus, you might have a group of all green things and a group of insects. Some of the insects will also be members of the group of green things and some of the green things will be insects. Got it? Furthermore, some categories may only have one member. For example, you are the sole member of the category of people who are identical to you. Who is identical to you? No one but you! That makes you very special indeed!

One of the central benefits of categorical logic, aside from its simplicity, is that it generates new knowledge. That is, by knowing one thing about the world, you can know more. If you know that all dogs are mammals, then you also know that the claim "some dogs are not mammals" is false.

Categorical logic deals with **categorical statements**. A categorical statement is a claim about the relationship between two groups of things. Here are a few examples:

> All kittens are cute.
> Some Canadians are good hockey players.
> No planets in our solar system hold alien life.

Each of these statements expresses a relationship between two groups of things; for example, the first sentence tells us that all members of the group "kittens" are also members of the group of "cute" things. In each of the above examples, the first group mentioned (kittens, Canadians, planets in our solar system) is the **subject** of the categorical statement, while the second group mentioned (cute, good hockey players, thing holding alien life) is the **predicate**. In other words, every categorical statement tells us something about the relationship between a subject group and a predicate group.

In categorical logic there are four possible relationships between groups. If S stands for the subject of a categorical statement, and P stands for the predicate, then you can have four (of what is referred to as) *statement forms*: **A**, **E**, **I**, and **O**. Don't worry about what the A, E, I, O stand for, but do notice that they are easy to remember because they are all (coincidentally) vowels.

> A statement form: All S are P.
> E statement form: No S are P.
> I statement form: Some S are P.
> O statement form: Some S are not P.

Thus, you could claim that all snakes are poisonous, or no snakes are poisonous, or some snakes are poisonous, or some snakes are not poisonous.

There are numerous ways to say statements of the A, E, I, and O forms. It can be helpful to translate these statements into a uniform style so that they can be more easily categorized as A, E, I, or O.

Every dog is a mammal. = "All dogs are mammals." (A)

If it is a dog, then it is a mammal. = "All dogs are mammals." (A)

Each and every piece of luggage cannot be more than 10 kilograms to be taken on the plane. = "No pieces of luggage that will be taken on the plane are more than 10 kilograms." (E)

None of the guests left the party early. = "No guests are among those who left the party early." (E)

Most cats are cuddly. = "Some cats are cuddly" (I)

Many children like school. = "Some children are among those who like school." (I)

Almost all kids don't like broccoli. = "Some kids are not among those who like broccoli." (O)

34% of people did not vote in the last election. = "Some people are not among those who voted in the last election." (O)

Although most of the above are pretty straightforward, there are some tricky translations. For example, "Only" does not mean "All." "Only people from the prairies are farmers" does not mean that "All people from the prairies are farmers." Rather, it means that if the person is a farmer, then he or she is from the prairies. Here you must switch the location of the subject and predicate terms to create the correct sentence of the A statement form.

Only S are P = "All P are S"

This is more obvious with some statements than with others. Take the statement "Only women give birth," for example. The correct form, "All people who give birth are women" is correct, but "All women give birth" clearly isn't! As well, be careful with statements that sound singular but aren't.

A dog is a mammal. = "All dogs are mammals" (statement form A).

But

A friend came over today. = "Some of my friends came over today" (statement form I).

E Statement:
A categorical statement of the form "No S are P." This states that no members of S are members of P. Also called a "universal negative."

I Statement:
A categorical statement of the form "Some S are P." This states that there exists at least one member of S that is also a member of P. Also called a "particular affirmative."

O Statement:
A categorical statement of the form "Some S are not P." This states that there exists at least one member of S that is not also a member of P. Also called a "particular negative."

Also be careful about potentially ambiguous statements. How would you translate "Nurses are caring professionals"? Should you translate it to the A statement form or the I statement form? For help, look to the context and consider which is more likely the intended meaning.

Some Peculiarities of Categorical Statements

Note that categorical statements cannot capture all of the nuances of our language. "A friend" is translated in exactly the same way as "a few friends" or "most friends"— any part of a group greater than none and less than all is translated as "some."

Consider the statement: "Plato was the author of *The Republic*." How would you translate this into categorical form?

"Some P are R"?

No, you want the famous philosopher Plato, not "some Platos" or "some people."

"All P are R"?

Since an individual is not a group, but rather a category of one, you need to treat the statement as "All persons identical to Plato are the authors of the *Republic*." "All P are R" is right, but it is right only when you intend the P to refer to the category of "persons identical to Plato," which is quite awkward!

Another tricky aspect of categorical statements is the relationship between "All" and "Some" statements. For ancients logicians, A and E statements also entailed that their subjects existed. If "All S are P," then surely "Some S must be P" too. This makes sense, doesn't it? If all dogs are mammals, then some dogs must be mammals! (In fact, there's even a name for this relation: "sub-alternation.") However, many modern logicians don't agree with this. A and E statements refer to their subjects such that *if* there is an S, *then* it is a P. Thus, the warning that "All students who cheat will fail the course" is true even if there are no students who actually cheat. But since I and O statements refer to existing particulars—"some" means at least one—you can't move from A to I or from E to O. Sometimes such inferences make sense, other times not. That "All dogs are mammals" must entail that "Some dogs are mammals." Yet "All vampires are sexy creatures" cannot entail that "Some vampires are sexy"— because there are none. In this book, we'll stick to the modern model, according to which we cannot infer I and O statements from their A and E equivalents.

Square of Opposition:
A graphic representation of the logical relationships between the four types of categorical statement.

7.2 The Square of Opposition

You can plot much of the information you require for this chapter onto the **Square of Opposition**. It is called this because the information in the opposite diagonal corners is ... opposite! A is the opposite of O and E is the opposite of I.

A	E
All S are P	*No S are P*
• Universal Affirmative	• Universal Negative
• S is distributed	• S is distributed
• P is undistributed	• P is distributed
I	**O**
Some S are P	*Some S are Not P*
• Particular Affirmative	• Particular Negative
• S is undistributed	• S is undistributed
• P is undistributed	• P is distributed

A and E statements are both **universal**. This just means that they say something about all members of the subject category. A statements say that all members of the subject category *are* members of the predicate category (and so they are "affirmative"), while E statements say that all members of the subject category *are not* members of the predicate category (and so they are "negative"). I and O statements, on the other hand, are **particular** in that they say something about *some but not all* members of the subject category.

A and E statements are **contraries**. For any given subject and predicate, A and E cannot both be true at the same time, but both can be false at the same time:

A: All the flowers are pretty. E: None of the flowers are pretty.

These claims could not both be true. But both of these claims could be false; for example, some of the flowers could be pretty and the others could be plain or ugly.

I and O are **sub-contraries**. For any subject and predicate, I and O cannot both be false at the same time, but both can be true at the same time:

I: Some horses are fast. O: Some horses are not fast.

Both of these claims could be true at the same time—some horses could be fast and others not, and that would make logical sense. However, that "some horses are fast" does not necessarily allow you to conclude that "some horses are not fast"—maybe *all* horses are fast, in which case it would also be true that "some" of them are fast. So be very careful not to assume that just because an I statement is true, the corresponding O statement is also true (or, for that matter, false). All you can claim is that the truth of an I statement leaves the truth or falsity of an O statement unknown.

The pair A and O, and the pair E and I are **contradictories**. If one is true, the other is false and vice versa. If "all dogs are mammals" is true, then "some dogs are not mammals" must be false (and vice versa). If the claim that "no one came to my party" is true, then the claim that "someone did come to my party" must be false.

Universal Statement: A categorical statement that describes a property of all members of the subject category.

Particular Statement: A categorical statement that describes a property of some (but not all) members of the subject category.

Contraries: Categorical statements that can both be false at the same time but cannot both be true at the same time. Statements of the A and E forms are contrary to one another.

Sub-Contraries: Categorical statements that can both be true at the same time but cannot both be false at the same time. Statements of the I and O forms are sub-contrary to one another.

Contradictories: Categorical statements in a pair such that if one is true, the other must be false, and vice versa. Statements of the A and O forms are contrary to one another; so are statements of the E and I forms.

Distribution: A property of categories within categorical statements. A category is distributed within a categorical statement if the statement indicates something about each and every member of that category. The subject category is distributed in A and E statements; the predicate category is distributed in E and O statements.

In the Square of Opposition above there is a philosophy term you might not have come across before: **distributed**. Don't be afraid of it. In any categorical statement, a category is distributed if the statement tells you something about each and every member of that category. For example, consider the A statement "All dogs are mammals." This statement tells you something about each and every member of the category "dogs" (namely, that they are all mammals). So "dogs" is distributed in the statement "All dogs are mammals." Does the statement tell you something about all mammals? No; you know that some mammals are dogs, but there are lots of other kinds of mammal. So "mammals" is undistributed in "All dogs are mammals." In other words, in the statement "All dogs are mammals," the subject ("dogs") is distributed while the predicate ("mammals") is not. And the same is true for any statement of the A statement form.

Take the E statement "No members of the Blue Bombers are members of the Argonauts." Does this statement tell you something about all the Blue Bomber players? Yes, that none of them play for the Toronto Argonauts. So the subject of the E statement form "No B are T" is distributed. Does the statement tell you something about all of the Argos? Yes, that none of them play for Winnipeg. So the predicate is also distributed in this statement. In the statement "No members of the Blue Bombers are members of the Argonauts," as with any E statement, both the subject and the predicate are distributed.

Now let's consider the I statement "Some shirts are plaid." This statement does not say anything about all shirts, or about all plaid things. It is telling you about only *some* members of the subject category and some members of the predicate category. So, in an I statement, neither category is distributed.

Finally, consider the O statement "Some snowmen are not pretty." This statement refers only to some snowmen, not all of them—with an O statement the subject is undistributed, as the statement does not say anything about all members of the subject group. But it *does* tell you something about all members of the predicate category. It tells you that if you have something that is pretty, it is not going to be among the "some snowmen" that are not pretty. This is a very tricky point to grasp, but suffice it to say that in an O statement, the subject is undistributed and the predicate is distributed.

Logically Equivalent Statements: Statements that are true and false under the same conditions—meaning that they could both be true or both be false, but if one were true the other could not be false. For example, "All S are P" is logically equivalent to "No S are not P."

7.3 Rules of Inference

Rules of inference come into play when a categorical statement is **logically equivalent** to another categorical statement. Two statements are logically equivalent when they are true or false under the same conditions. In other words, they are equivalent if it's impossible for one to be true and the other false.

Consider some examples. If "No dogs are animals that meow" is true, then it follows that "No animal that meows is a dog." Do you see why? If you have a dog, you know it isn't going to meow. So if you are told that there is something meowing, you know it isn't going to be a dog. This works for some other types of categorical statements too. If you know that "Some dogs are friendly," then you can immediately conclude that "Some friendly animals are dogs." However, this doesn't apply to all statement forms. If you know that "All dogs are mammals" is true, you cannot switch the subject and predicate and conclude that "All mammals are dogs." *Some* mammals are dogs, certainly, but there are also giraffes and cats and elephants.

Conversion

To **convert** a categorical statement, you switch the subject and predicate. S becomes P, P becomes S.

> E: "No S are G" = "No G are S"
> Example: If "No spiders are good swimmers," then it follows that anything that is a good swimmer is not going to be a spider ("No good swimmers are spiders").

> I: "Some S are P" = "Some P are S"
> Example: If "Some spiders are poisonous," then "Some poisonous things are spiders."

Only E and I statements can be converted. If you attempt to convert an A or O statement, you'll end up with two statements that are not logically equivalent:

> A: "All S are P" *does not equal* "All P are S"
> Example: "All spiders are small" *does not* mean the same thing as "All small things are spiders"—one of these can be true and the other false.

> O: "Some T are not A" *does not equal* "Some A are not T"
> Example: "Some spiders are not black widows" *does not* mean the same thing as "Some black widows are not spiders."

Obversion

Obversion involves two steps:

1. Switch the scope with its opposite: "All" becomes "No"; "No" becomes "All"; "Some ... are" becomes "Some ... are not"; "Some ... are not" becomes "Some ... are."
2. Change the predicate to its **complement**. The complement of P is non-P (everything that is not a P), and the complement of non-P is P.

All statement forms can be transformed into their logical equivalents by obversion.

> A: "All S are P." Therefore, "No S are non-P."
> Step 1: Switch the scope: *No* S are P.
> Step 2: Change the predicate to its complement: No S are *non-P*.

Conversion: A logical operation performed on a categorical statement by switching the subject and the predicate. Only E and I statements can be converted while staying logically equivalent.

Obversion: A logical operation in which the scope of a categorical statement is switched (from positive to negative or from negative to positive) and "non-" is added to the predicate. All obverted statements are logically equivalent to their originals.

Complement: The opposite of a given category. For example, the complement of the category "eagles" is "non-eagles" (everything that is not an eagle).

Example: "All elephants are big" = "No elephants are non-big"—both of these statements mean the same thing, and so the original statement and its obversion are logically equivalent.

E: No S are P. Therefore, All S are non-P.
Example: "No reality television programs are non-scripted." = "All reality television programs are scripted."

I: Some S are P. Therefore, Some S are not non-P.
Example: "Some television shows are informative." = "Some television shows are not non-informative."

O: Some S are not P. Therefore, Some S are non-P.
Example: "Some rational animals are not human." = "Some rational animals are non-human." (Remember, you can obvert a categorical statement regardless of whether you believe it is true!)

Contraposition

Contraposition involves two steps:
1. Convert S and P; that is, exchange them with one another.
2. Replace the subject and the predicate with their respective complements.

Only statements of the A and O forms can be legitimately transformed by contraposition.

A: All S are P.
    Step 1: Convert: All P are S.
    Step 2: Replace subject and predicate with complements: All non-P are non-S.
Example: "All fish are swimmers" = "All non-swimmers are non-fish" (anything that can't swim isn't a fish).

O: Some S are not P.
    Step 1: Convert: Some P are not S.
    Step 2: Replace subject and predicate with complements: Some non-P are not non-S.
Example: "Some Albertans are not ranchers" = "Some non-ranchers are not non-Albertans" (i.e., there is at least one person who is not a rancher but is an Albertan).

The operations performed here create some odd sounding statements, and it's not always obvious whether two statements are logically equivalent. But when you translate the resulting statements further into (or back into) ordinary language, it may be easier to see what they mean and determine which of them are logically equivalent. Appreciating the rules of inference allows you to understand the strict logic behind deductive reasoning, whether you're assessing or creating arguments.

Contraposition:
A logical operation in which a categorical statement is converted (its subject and predicate are reversed) and "non-" is attached to both categories.

7.4 Depicting Categorical Statements Using Venn Diagrams

Every categorical statement can be represented visually using **Venn diagrams**. Two intersecting circles represent the possible relationships between the subject group and the predicate group. The intersection (noted by C below) represents shared or common features between the two groups. So, for example, suppose that in the diagram below the circle on the left is populated with snakes and the circle on the right is populated with things that are poisonous. Area C would contain all snakes that are poisonous. Accordingly, the remaining area on the left, A, would be non-poisonous snakes (e.g., common garden snakes and more), and the remaining area on the right, B, would be poisonous things that are not snakes, such as poisonous plants and chemicals.

Venn Diagram:
A diagram of overlapping circles representing a relationship between two or more categories.

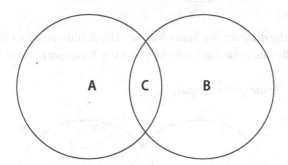

Below is the diagram representing *All S are P*. S is the subject, P is the predicate. All of the area of S that is outside of P has been shaded, indicating that it is empty. There cannot be anything that is an S that is not a P.

Example: "All Swiss watches are precise instruments."

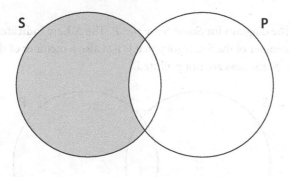

Below is the diagram for *No S are P*. The area of S that overlaps with P is shaded in to indicate that it is empty. There is no member of S that is also a member of P. Example: "No soldiers are pacifists."

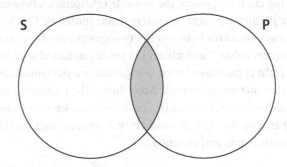

Below is the diagram for *Some S are P*. The X indicates that there is something that falls into both the S category and the P category. There is at least one S that is also a P.

Example: "Some shirts are purple."

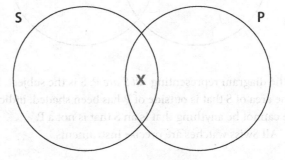

Below is the diagram for *Some S are not P*. The X here indicates that there is at least one member of the S category that is not also a member of the P category. Example: "Some seas are not polluted."

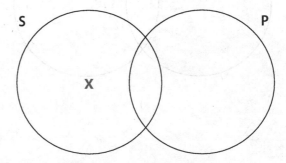

So far, we've looked at what categorical statements are and how they can be represented using Venn diagrams. But the real reason why categorical statements are interesting is that they can be used to represent and assess arguments. In the remainder of this chapter, we'll look at two different techniques for assessing arguments using categorical logic—one using Venn diagrams and the other using a list of rules that functions as a test of validity.

7.5 Categorical Syllogisms

When you combine three categorical statements to create an argument, the argument you come up with is a **Categorical syllogism**. These are distinguished from other types of arguments in that they always have exactly *two premises, one conclusion, and three categories, and they use each category only twice.* These terms are called:

1. The **minor term** (the subject of the conclusion)
2. The **major term** (the predicate of the conclusion)
3. The **middle term** (the term that appears only in the premises)

Consider, for example, the following argument:

P1) All A's (minor term) are B's (middle term).
P2) All B's (middle term) are C (major term).
_____
C3) Therefore, all A's (minor term) are C (major term).

Suppose we have a categorical syllogism in which the three categories are "planets in our solar system" (middle term), "planets that hold alien life" (major term), and "planets that we can travel to" (minor term). The argument is this:

P1) No planets in our solar system (middle) hold alien life (major).
P2) All planets that we can travel to (minor) are in our solar system (middle).
_____
C3) Therefore, no planet that we can travel to (minor) holds alien life (major).

To evaluate a categorical syllogism, what you need to do first is translate the argument into a series of A, E, I, and/or O statements, which we've discussed above. Then, you need to use one of the techniques described below to determine whether the conclusion can be drawn from the two premises. If it can, then the argument is deductively valid.

Categorical Syllogism: A form of argument in which one categorical statement is deduced from two other categorical statements.

Minor Term: In a categorical syllogism, the subject of the conclusion.

Major Term: In a categorical syllogism, the predicate in the conclusion.

Middle Term: In a categorical syllogism, the term that appears in both premises but not the conclusion.

7.6 Using Venn Diagrams to Evaluate Categorical Syllogisms

One of the easiest ways to test the pattern of a categorical syllogism is to draw the argument in the form of a Venn diagram. How this works is quite straightforward. Since every categorical syllogism includes three categories, each of which occurs in a premise or conclusion exactly twice, the test for validity of these types of arguments requires three overlapping circles, as shown below.

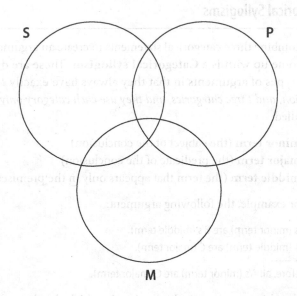

Assign the term for each of these categories to a circle. Then proceed to fill in the circles with shading or X's, using the information in the premises, in accordance with the diagrams in the previous section. Now look to the conclusion and see which X's or shading it would require; if that information has already been filled in by the premises, then the argument is valid. If the conclusion would require additional X's or shading, or if it contradicts the X's and shading that you've already filled in, then the argument is invalid. We'll go over this in more detail, with a few examples, in the following section.

Steps for Evaluating Categorical Syllogisms Using Venn Diagrams

1. Always draw your three overlapping circles so that they look like the outline of Mickey Mouse.
2. Always represent the minor term (subject of the conclusion) in the left circle, the major term (predicate of the conclusion) in the right circle, and the middle term (term only in the premises) in the middle (bottom) circle.

3. *Draw in the information contained in both premises on the diagram.
    Always represent universal statements first.* In other words, shade *out*
    areas first. Shading means that you are getting rid of an area; a shaded
    area has nothing in it. Once you've represented all of the universal
    premises (if there are any), fill in the particular premises by drawing
    X's in the appropriate areas. Remember that an X means that an area
    is *not* empty. If, when filling in the information for a particular state-
    ment, there is not enough information to determine which of two
    areas are populated, you should put an X on the line between those
    two areas. One tip that might help is to place the appropriate two-
    circle diagrams for each premise beside the three-circle diagram, then
    simply copy the information from the diagrams for premise 1 and
    premise 2 into the three circle diagram.

4. *Check to see if the conclusion has been represented.* If, by drawing in the
    two premises, you have represented what the conclusion should look
    like, then the argument is valid. If you have the represented additional
    information, that's fine. If the conclusion has not been drawn in, or if
    the information that has been drawn in contradicts the information in
    the conclusion, then the argument is invalid.

Here are a few examples:

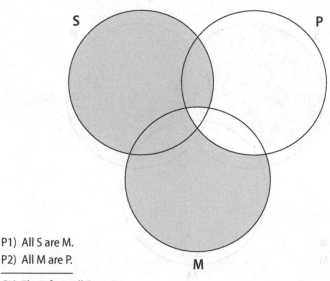

P1) All S are M.
P2) All M are P.
———————
C3) Therefore, all S are P.

By shading in the appropriate areas for the two premises, you can see that the
conclusion has been drawn in as well. Therefore, this argument is valid.

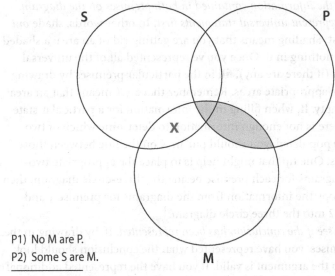

P1) No M are P.
P2) Some S are M.
_____
C3) Therefore, some S are not P.

By shading in the area of M that overlaps P, and then putting an X in the only space left open that is shared by S and M, you can see that there is an X in S but outside of P. Therefore, the conclusion has been established by the premises. The argument is valid.

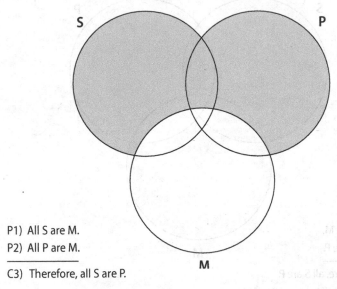

P1) All S are M.
P2) All P are M.
_____
C3) Therefore, all S are P.

Here you'll note that only a portion of S has been shaded out. To represent the conclusion, you'd have to shade out an additional area of S, so as to indicate that there are not some things that are S but not P. Therefore, the argument is invalid.

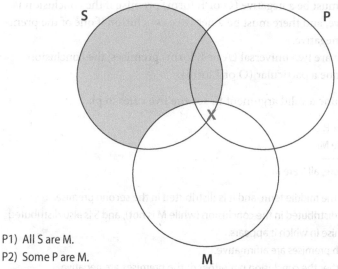

P1) All S are M.

P2) Some P are M.

_____

C3) Therefore, some S are P.

In this example, we begin as usual by shading out the area represented by the universal premise. However, even after the shading, there are two areas within P and M; because you are not given any further information in the second premise, the X must go on the line that bisects the areas between P and M. The reason for this is clear. If you put the X in the area where all three circles overlap, then you would be stating that Some P are M *and* are also S. But you do not know that this is true. So if you did this, you would be stating more than you actually know. Likewise, if you put the X in the area between P and M but outside the S circle, you would be saying that Some P are M *but are not* S. Again, you don't know whether this is true or not. Because you do not know if the X is in S, the conclusion has not been shown by the premises. The argument is therefore invalid.

7.7 Using Rules to Evaluate Categorical Syllogisms

What's nice about categorical logic is that there's another way to check your arguments for deductive validity, aside from Venn diagrams.

You may apply the following rules to determine if a categorical syllogism is valid:

1. The middle term, which is in both premises but not the conclusion, must be distributed at least once.
2. If a term is distributed in the conclusion, it must be distributed in a premise.
3. There must be at least one affirmative premise (i.e., a statement of the A or I form).

4. There must be a negative (O or E form) premise if the conclusion is negative, and there must be a negative conclusion if one of the premises is negative.
5. If there are two universal (A or E form) premises, the conclusion cannot be a particular (O or I form).

Let's examine a valid argument to see the five rules in play.

P1) All S are P.
P2) All P are M.

_____

C3) Therefore, all S are M.

Rule 1. P is the middle term, and it is distributed in the second premise.
Rule 2. S is distributed in the conclusion (while M is not), and S is also distributed in the premise in which it appears.
Rule 3. Both premises are affirmative.
Rule 4. Neither the conclusion nor either of the premises are negative.
Rule 5. The two premises are universal, and the conclusion is as well.

Rule 5 is pretty easy to grasp if you think about Venn diagrams. If you had two universals, you would be shading out parts of the diagram. If the conclusion were a particular, you would be looking for an X, but you wouldn't have put one anywhere. Likewise, if you had two particular premises and put X's down, and the conclusion was a universal, this too would be invalid since you would not have any parts of the diagram shaded.

Here's another valid categorical syllogism.

P1) No M are P.
P2) Some S are M.

_____

C3) Therefore, some S are not P.

Rule 1. M is the middle term because it is in both premises and not the conclusion. It is distributed in the first premise.
Rule 2. In the conclusion, S is not distributed and P is distributed. P is also distributed in the first premise.
Rule 3. The second premise is an I statement form, so it is affirmative.
Rule 4. There is a negative premise and a negative conclusion.
Rule 5. The conclusion is a particular and there is a particular premise.
Therefore, the argument adheres to all five rules and is valid.

Missing Statements

As you know by now, sometimes people leave out bits of their arguments. If a categorical syllogism has an implicit premise or conclusion, you can combine your knowledge of what a categorical syllogism is (i.e., three statements and three categories, each mentioned only twice) with the five rules above to determine what the missing statement is. This won't work in all cases (as you'll see below), but more often than not we can use this technique to fill out incomplete syllogisms. The only potential concern here is that you have to assume that the argument is valid. If the argument is invalid, and the missing premise wasn't intended, then you will not be able to use this technique without misrepresenting the argument. The rule of thumb, however, is to be nice and assume that a valid categorical syllogism was intended.

P1) All humans are mortal.
P2) All mortal things are things that die.

_____

Therefore, ?

"Humans" and "things that die" appear only once in our argument, so they must be the missing categories in the conclusion. Since you cannot move from two affirmative premises to a negative conclusion, and you cannot move from two universal statements to a particular, the conclusion must be an affirmative universal statement. This entails that it must be an A statement. But where do the categories fit? Which one is the subject and which is the predicate? Well, since the subject of an A statement is distributed, while the predicate is not, we know (according to Rule 2) that the subject of this argument's conclusion must be distributed in one of the premises. "Humans" is distributed in the first premise, while "things that die" is not distributed in the second premise, so "humans" must be the subject of the conclusion. Thus, the conclusion can only be "All humans are things that die."

P1) No B are C.
P2) All A are C.

_____

C3) Therefore, ?

In order for this argument to be valid, you know that the conclusion has to contain A and B, since C is already mentioned twice. The premises are both universal, so the conclusion must be as well, according to Rule 5. There is a negative premise, so the conclusion must also be negative, according to Rule 4. This means the missing conclusion must be a universal negative statement—it must be of the E form. But is it "No A are B" or "No B are A"? Both the subject and the predicate are distributed in the E statement form, so Rule 2 doesn't help. In fact, the rules give us more than one answer: "No A are B" and "No B are A" are *both* valid conclusions to this argument! This might be surprising until you realize that the two statements are logically equivalent—we can go from one to the other using conversion. So either one is a valid conclusion to this argument.

P1) All R are P.
?

_____

C3) Therefore, some P are Q.

P is already mentioned twice, so that means the missing premise has R and Q in it. Both statements that are provided are affirmative, so the missing one must also be affirmative. You cannot move from two universals to a particular conclusion, so you need a particular premise. Thus you are left with "Some R are Q" (or its equivalent, "Some Q are R," since either premise leads to a valid argument).

7.8 Chapter Exercises

Exercise 7.1

TRUE/FALSE QUESTIONS

1. Of the four forms of categorical statement, if A is true, then E is false, I is true, and O is false. True or False?
2. Of the four forms of categorical statement, if E is true, then A is false, I is false, and O is true. True or False?
3. Of the four forms of categorical statement, if I is true, then A is undetermined, E is false, and O is undetermined. True or False?
4. Of the four forms of categorical statement, if O is true, then A is false, E is undetermined, and I is undetermined. True or False?
5. A category is distributed in a categorical statement if the statement tells you something about some members of that category. True or False?

Exercise 7.2

Determine whether the following arguments are valid or invalid using the five rules for categorical syllogisms.

1. P1) No N are Q.
   P2) All Q are Z.
   _____
   C3) Therefore, all Z are N.

2. P1) All T are W.
   P2) Some U are not T.
   _____
   C3) Therefore, no U are W.

3. Every voter is a citizen, but some citizens are not residents. Therefore, some voters are not residents.
4. No computer CDs contain data, and this is true because none of them are formatted and only formatted CDs contain data.
5. Not all supervisors are competent. No competent people were fired last week. Therefore, only supervisors were fired last week.

Exercise 7.3

What is the missing premise or conclusion in these valid categorical syllogisms?
Some may have multiple possible answers.

1. ?

   P2) All E are D.
   _____

   C3) Therefore, all E are I.

2. P1) No F are M.

   ?
   _____

   C3) Therefore, no H are M.

3. P1) All B are C.

   P2) Some B are A.
   _____

   C3) Therefore, ?

4. P1) Some A are not C.

   P2) All A are D.
   _____

   C3) Therefore, ?

5. All D are C.

   All A are D.
   _____

   Therefore, ?

Exercise 7.4

Look around you and select three categories of objects (e.g., people wearing black
shoes, spiral notebooks, blue pens) to create a valid categorical syllogism with
satisfactory premises, that is, a sound deductive argument.

For example, if you see that:

No people using blue pens are writing in spiral notebooks.

And you see that:

Some people wearing black shoes are using blue pens.

Then you now also know that:

Some people wearing black shoes are not writing in spiral notebooks.

Exercise 7.5

Create a satisfactory categorical statement for each of the A, E, I, O statement forms. For the A and E statements, determine what the contraries and contradictories would be. For the I and O statements, determine what the sub-contraries and contradictories would be. Are these new statements true, are they false, or is it not possible to determine whether they are true or false?

Exercise 7.6

The five arguments below are all valid categorical syllogisms. Determine which forms (A, E, I, O) are being used for each statement. Construct Venn diagrams to verify their validity. Finally, replace the variables M, P, and S with actual categories (e.g., Medical supplies, Polar bears, Sarcastic salespeople), making sure that all of the premises are satisfactory according to the S-Test. The resulting arguments will be deductively sound.

1. No M are P. All S are M. Therefore, no S are P.
2. No P are M. Some S are M. Therefore, some S are not P.
3. Some M are not P. All M are S. Therefore, some S are not P.
4. All M are P. Some S are M. Therefore, some S are P.
5. All M are P. All S are M. Therefore, all S are P.

7.9 Postscript

In this chapter, the logical relationships between different categories or groups of things was presented. Knowing one thing about the world allows you to also know more. You might not tell your friends to wait a few minutes for your rebuttal while you literally sketch out a diagram of their argument, but the logic discussed in this chapter reveals how premises and conclusions should fit together, with logical exactness, in some forms of deductive reasoning.

Don't worry if you find the Venn diagrams complicated. Just remember to deal with two circles at a time when plotting the information. Never diagram in the conclusion, since the point is to see whether the premises demonstrate the conclusion on their own; once you have diagrammed the two premises, look to see if the conclusion is represented. Anything more is okay (i.e., the argument is still valid even if it shows more than the conclusion); anything less or anything contradictory is not okay (i.e., it shows the argument is invalid).

You can use the Five Rules for Categorical Syllogisms to double-check your Venn diagrams, and vice versa. If you determined an argument was valid with one method and invalid with another, then you need to check where you went wrong.

The categorical logic presented in this chapter is useful for any argument that fits a certain form, specifically any deductive argument in which two categorical statements are used to prove another categorical statement. But as we've already seen in earlier chapters, there are many deductive arguments that don't fit this form. In the final chapter of this book, we'll examine a different form of logic that can be used to test the validity of some of the deductive arguments for which categorical logic is ill-suited.

CHAPTER 8

Propositional Logic Using Truth Tables

The categorical logic that we examined in the last chapter cannot capture all of the meaningful statements that people use in arguments. For example, none of the following sentences can be translated into categorical statements:

She is not going to the party unless she can find someone to work her shift at the hospital.

Nuclear power is safe, provided that all precautions are taken.

Either I will go to school or I will go back to bed and try to get rid of this cold.

This chapter will provide you with basic tools and skills to examine ordinary language with a mathematical degree of precision. It should also remind you how important the right words and the construction of statements are, especially when you are making or considering an argument—small changes in language can mean big changes in meaning.

Though propositional logic is more broadly applicable than the categorical logic discussed in the previous chapter, its use is limited to assessing sufficiency and support in some cases of deductive reasoning. This means that propositional logic can't be applied to inductive arguments, arguments from analogy, or to certain types of deductive arguments, which can't be adequately described using the tools discussed in this chapter. Furthermore, on its own, propositional logic can't show you whether or not a deductive argument is successful; to know that, you would also need to evaluate the satisfactoriness of the premises. When evaluating the satisfactoriness of premises, or when looking at inductive arguments and arguments from analogy, we must rely on the tools discussed in earlier chapters. 149

8.1 Translating Statements

Propositional Logic:
A type of symbolic logic that deals with the relationships between propositions using the basic logical connectives: 'and', 'or', 'not', and 'if ..., then'.

Logical Connective:
A word or symbol that relates one statement to another or to itself. Not, and, v, and → are all logical connectives.

Variable: A capital letter used in propositional logic to represent a proposition.

Propositional logic uses the **logical connectives** "not," "and," "or," and "if, then" to relate propositions to each other. Here are some ordinary sentences that use logical connectives:

> *If* it is raining outside, *then* I will need an umbrella.

> Newspapers need to figure out how to compete in the age of the Internet *or* they will go bankrupt.

> Walter wanted to play the roles of both King Lear *and* Othello in the upcoming productions of Shakespeare's plays.

> It is *not* a good day for hiking.

In many examples given throughout this book, we have used an uppercase letter to represent true or false statements or propositions. These letters are known as variables. The first step in evaluating an argument using propositional logic is to choose a variable to represent each one of the statements; you might choose the letter A for "Apples are good for you," B for "Bananas are yellow," and so forth. It does not matter which letter you select, but it is usually best that you choose something that will help you remember what the original proposition is. It can also be helpful to capitalize the letter that you've chosen when writing a statement out in English—for example:

> F: wood is Flammable.

Once you have translated an argument's statements into variables, then you need to translate its logical connectives. Each logical connective is represented by a symbol:

> Use a tilde for NOT (~),

> Use an ampersand for AND (&),

> Use a small letter v for OR (v),

> Use an arrow for IF, THEN (→)

Negation: A statement of the form "Not P." A negation is true if and only if the statement it negates is false. For example, "It is not the case that the Indian Ocean is the largest ocean on Earth."

Negation: Not (~)

> D = Dinosaurs once roamed the earth.

> ~D = It is not the case that dinosaurs once roamed the earth.

"It is not sunny outside" is a **negation** of the sentence "It is sunny outside"; if one is true, then the other must be false. Whatever truth value a statement has, that statement's negation has the opposite truth value.

Conjunction: And (&)

B & R = I am bored and I want to go for a run.

An "and" statement, or **conjunction,** is true only if both of the statements it connects are true. For example, the statement above is true only if it is true that "I am bored" *and* it is true that "I want to go for a run." The "and" of propositional logic does not say there is any real relationship between propositions P and Q, whereas in ordinary usage we tend to join statements together only if they are related or relevant to each other. That is, you might say, "I am going to university and I am working part time as well." But "P & Q" could also be "I am going to university and potato chips come in many flavours."

"And" can also be used in everyday language to represent a time relationship. In other words, "and" can mean "and then." "I am going to the store and the gas station" normally means "I am going to the store and then to the gas station." Common sense tells us you cannot go to two places at the same time. However, the "and" of propositional logic does not say anything about time, and the truth value for "T & B" will be the same as that for "B & T," just as in mathematics, where "2 × 3" is the same as "3 × 2."

Other words with the same meaning in propositional logic as "and" include "but" and "although," even though these words sometimes have different implications in English.

T & R = I am Tired but want to go for a Run.

T & S = I am Tired although I got lots of Sleep last night.

Disjunction: Or (v)

I v U = I'm going to stay Indoors today or I'm going to carry an Umbrella.

H v P = My computer needs a new Hard drive or it needs a new Processor.

An "or" statement, or **disjunction,** is true when either of the propositions connected to it are true or when both are true. So, in the second example above, "H v P" is true if I only need a new hard drive (and not a new processor), or if I only need a new processor (and not a new hard drive)—but it's also true if I need both a new hard drive and a new processor. When someone gives you an option of A or B in this sense, it is possible that both options are viable.

"Do you want cream or sugar in your coffee?" "Yes. Both please!"

Sometimes, in ordinary language, we use the word "or" to connect two propositions that can't both be true at the same time, as in "You can either keep the money or you can risk it all to try to win the jackpot!" But this is not how we're using "v" in propositional logic; here, a disjunction is true if the statements on either side of the "or" are both true.

Conjunction: A statement of the form "P and Q." A conjunction connects two other statements such that it is true if and only if the connected statements are true. For example, "Penguins are birds and dogs are mammals."

Disjunction: A statement of the form "P or Q." A disjunction connects two other statements such that it is true if and only if one or both of the connected statements are true. For example, "Either penguins can fly or sparrows can fly."

Conditional: If, then (→)

> D → M = If Herman is a Dog, then Herman is a Mammal.
>
> N → F = If the Newspaper publishes my story, I'll be Famous!

Conditional Statement: A statement of the form "If P, then Q." A conditional does not assert that P actually is the case but rather states that if P is the case then Q must be also.

Antecedent: The first proposition in an "If ..., then ..." statement (a conditional statement), immediately following the "If." In the conditional statement "If P, then Q," P is the antecedent.

Consequent: The second proposition in an "If ..., then ..." conditional statement, immediately following the "then." In the conditional statement "If P, then Q," Q is the consequent.

"If, then" statements are more commonly referred to as hypothetical or **conditional statements**. A conditional statement claims that *if* something is true, *then* something else is also true. The "if, then" symbol "→" goes between two propositions. The proposition before the → is called the **antecedent**, while the proposition after the → is called the **consequent**: "antecedent → consequent." Thus,

> S → C = *If* it is Snowing, *then* it is Cold outside.

"It is Snowing" is the antecedent; "it is Cold outside" is the consequent.

Some Tricky "If, Then" Translations

In propositional logic, the order of "if, then" statements is important. When "if" is in the middle of a conditional statement, rather than at the beginning, it's a good idea to rearrange the statement. Consider the following example:

> It is Cold outside, *if* it is Snowing.

In this case, just pull "if" and what is behind it up to the front. Thus, the statement becomes

> If it is Snowing, then it is Cold outside.

or

> S → C

What about this next one?

> Unless it is Snowing, then it is Cold outside.

Here, treat "unless it is Snowing" as meaning "so long as it is not snowing" or "if it is not snowing." So you now get:

> ~S → C

"Implies" works just like "if, then." Thus, if your sentence was

> The fact that it is Snowing implies that it is Cold outside.

you get

> S → C

"Provided that" works much the same way as "if." Simply take everything after "provided that" to the start of the statement and add in the "if" and "then." So,

It is Snowing, provided that it is Cold outside.

becomes

If it is Cold outside, then it is Snowing.

which is written as

C → S

Complex Statements

Any statement that includes more than one logical connective is called a **complex statement**.

> Either it will be Sunny today or I will stay Inside and watch Television.
>
> If it Looks like a duck and it Walks like a duck, it's a Duck ... or a Goose.
>
> I like Scary movies, but *The Cabin in the Woods* just isn't scary.

To properly represent any one of these statements, we need to use at least two logical connective symbols. Let's try the first one:

> Either it will be sunny today or I will stay inside and watch television. = S v I & T
> (incorrect)

The problem here is that the translation is ambiguous. It could represent the intended meaning of the original English sentence, or it could mean something different: "It's either sunny today or I will stay inside. And I'm going to watch television." To eliminate the ambiguity, we'll add brackets.

Brackets work much like those used in mathematics to indicate order of operations. Consider this mathematical statement:

2 + 3 × 5 = ?

We can change the meaning of this formula by adding brackets, which indicate that the portion in brackets should be calculated before the rest of the equation:

2 + (3 × 5) = 17

(2 + 3) × 5 = 25

Similarly, the translation of the earlier English sentence is ambiguous until brackets are added:

S v (I & T)

With brackets, the translation is now unambiguous. It says that either it will be sunny or (I will stay inside and watch television). The bracketed part of the statement is called a **component statement**.

Complex Statement:
A statement that includes more than one logical connective.

Component Statement:
A statement that includes a logical connective and is embedded within a complex statement.

The second example includes two component statements:

If it Looks like a duck and it Walks like a duck, it's a Duck ... or a Goose.

(L & W) → (D v G)

The third case is another complex statement with a single component statement:

I like Scary movies, but *The Cabin in the Woods* just isn't scary.

S & ~C

You'll notice that there are no brackets in this translation, even though it's a complex statement. You can add brackets if you'd like, to make "S & (~C)," but this is not necessary. Unlike the other logical connectives, the negation symbol is applied to just one variable and so its meaning is unambiguous even without brackets.

Therefore

Every conclusion in the standardized arguments from previous chapters has started with "Therefore." This is intentional, for unlike other conclusion indicator words (So, Hence, Thus, etc.), there is a symbol we use in propositional logic for therefore: ∴

Truth Values and Validity

In propositional logic, every statement can only be true or false. The truth or falsity of a statement is its **truth value**. "Jean Chrétien was prime minister of Canada" has a truth value of "True," while "Most polar bears are herbivores" has a truth value of "False." But, as discussed in Chapter 5, you don't need to know whether the statements in an argument are true in order to tell whether the argument is valid—you only need to know whether the premises would support the conclusion *if they were all true.*

In the next few sections, you will learn to evaluate arguments using the truth table technique. This technique allows you to determine whether it is possible for a given argument to have all true premises and a false conclusion. If it is possible, then the argument is invalid because the conclusion is not established by the premises. The argument is valid, on the other hand, if it is impossible for its premises to be true while its conclusion is false.

Truth Value: The truth or falsity of a statement. For example, the truth value of the statement "Ontario is a province of Canada" is "True."

8.2 Basic Truth Tables for "And," "Or," "Not," and "If, Then"

Let's begin by plotting the truth values of some variables on a truth table. Every proposition is either true or false. Accordingly, if you have two propositions P and Q, there are four possible combinations of truth values. The first proposition could be true and the second false, both could be true, both could be false, or the first one could be false and the second one true.

There is a proper procedure to use in order to make sure you always capture all of the combinations. You first write down your variables in the order that they appear. Starting with the one on the right, you then put a column of T, F, T, F, immediately below the variable (T for True and F for false).

P	Q
	T
	F
	T
	F

You then move to the next variable on the left and fill that column with T's and F's. In this case, because there are only two variables, you put down two T's and two F's.

P	Q
T	T
T	F
F	T
F	F

You now have all the combinations that you need. In the first row above, P is true and Q is true; in the second row, P is true and Q is false; and so on.

If there are more than two variables, you can employ a similar procedure. For example, if there are three variables, then there are eight different possibilities, represented in the following way:

P	Q	R
T	T	T
T	T	F
T	F	T
T	F	F
F	T	T
F	T	F
F	F	T
F	F	F

Since each statement has two possible truth values (True and False), you can determine the number of rows you'll need using the formula 2n, where n = the number of variables. Thus, there will be four rows when there are two variables, eight rows when there are three variables, 16 rows when there are four variables, and so on.

Negation

We can extend the truth table to show the truth value of a statement that uses the logical connectives discussed above. The basic truth table for negation is the easiest. Whenever P is true, ~P is false. Whenever P is false, ~P is true. Thus, if "I will go to the park" is true, then "I will not go to the park" is false, and vice versa.

P	~P
T	F
F	T

Conjunction

Let's look at conjunction next. When you are figuring out the truth values for P & Q, you are determining when the entire conjunction is true. Consider:

Today is Tuesday and it is hot outside.

When is this true? Let P represent "Today is Tuesday" (best not to use T as a variable, since it also stands for True) and Q represent "It is hot outside." It must both be Tuesday and hot outside for the conjunction to be true. If it is Wednesday and hot, the entire sentence is false. If it is Tuesday and cold, the sentence is false. P and Q must both be true in order for the whole conjunction P & Q to be true. All other combinations are false.

Thus, your basic truth table for conjunction will look like this:

P	Q	P & Q
T	T	T
T	F	F
F	T	F
F	F	F

Disjunction

The disjunction of P v Q is only false when both propositions are false. Thus, "I will go to the park or I will go to the Queezy Mall" (P v Q) is true if I choose to do both. If I only go to the park, what I said is still true. If I just go to the Queezy Mall, it's still true. If I stay home instead and do not go to either place, then the statement is false. Here is the basic truth table for "or":

P	Q	P v Q
T	T	T
T	F	T
F	T	T
F	F	F

Conditional Statements

The truth table for conditional statements may be the most difficult to grasp. An "if, then" statement is claiming that if P is true, Q is also true. This *does not* mean that if P is false, Q will also be false. For example, suppose the statement "If I have a million dollars, then I will be happy" is true. I have a million dollars. So I am happy. But the statement doesn't say that I won't be happy if I don't have a million dollars. I can also be happy if I am in love, or healthy, or on holidays. The only combination that the statement doesn't allow is when I have a million dollars but I am not happy. In other words, the statement P → Q is false *only* if P is true and Q is false. Here is the truth table for the "if, then" conditional:

P	Q	P→Q
T	T	T
T	F	F
F	T	T
F	F	T

The last combination is the one that throws most people off. How can two falses make something true? But just think about the original claim. If I have a million dollars, then I will be happy. But I don't have a million dollars (P is false) and I am not happy (Q is false). Thus, the original claim is true!

8.3 Creating Long Truth Tables

Now let's look at how these truth tables can be used to determine the validity of arguments. There are five basic steps in what we will call the **long truth table method**:

1. Assign a variable to each of the claims in the argument. (e.g., A, T, Q, etc.)
2. Translate each statement of the argument using variables and logical connectives. (e.g., P → R)
3. Create the top line of a truth table by plotting the various components of the argument. These components include variables, premises, and at least one conclusion. Give each variable its own column, and if any of the premises or conclusion(s) are complex statements, then also give each of the component statements (including negations) its own column.
4. Fill in each row and column of the truth table. Be sure to begin with the possible truth values of the individual variables, then fill in the truth values of any component statements, and then finally the premises and the conclusion.
5. Once you have filled in the entire truth table, check to see if there is any combination where the premises are all true and the conclusion

Long Truth Table Method: The use of a chart to plot out all possible truth values of an argument's variables and statements in order to determine whether the argument is valid. If one or more rows in the table show the conclusion as false and all the premises as true, then the argument is invalid.

is false. If there is, then the argument is invalid since it is logically possible for the conclusion to be true and the premises false. If there is not, then the argument is valid since it is impossible for the premises to be true and the conclusion false.

Let's try an example.

If it is August, then it is Summer time. It is not August. Therefore, it is not Summer time.

First, determine the variable letters. Let A stand for "It is August" and S for "It is Summer time." Next, symbolize the argument:

P1) A → S
P2) ~A
_____

C3) ∴ ~S

Now create a truth table. At the top, place each variable in order of its appearance in the argument. Then create columns for the premises and the conclusion. The ordering of the premises and conclusion is not important, but it is useful to have a standard approach to laying these out (in this case, we've placed the negated statements to the left of the conditional because they are easier to assess). If a premise or conclusion is complex, you must create a separate column for each component statement. There are no complex statements in this argument, so that's not necessary here.

		Premise 2	Conclusion 3	Premise 1
A	**S**	**~A**	**~S**	**A → S**

Starting with the variable on the right (S), create a column alternating T (for true) and F (for false).

		Premise 2	Conclusion 3	Premise 1
A	**S**	**~A**	**~S**	**A → S**
	T			
	F			
	T			
	F			

Move to the next variable (closer to the left side) and alternate between pairs of T's and pairs of F's.

		Premise 2	Conclusion 3	Premise 1
A	**S**	**~A**	**~S**	**A → S**
T	T			
T	F			
F	T			
F	F			

Using the information that has now been plotted, plug in the appropriate truth value of either T or F in the columns for the premises and conclusion. That is, if A is true, ~A is false. If S is false, ~S is true. And, if A is true and S is true, then A → S is also true (using the basic truth table for conditional statements).

		Premise 2	Conclusion 3	Premise 1	
A	**S**	**~A**	**~S**	**A → S**	
T	T	F	F	T	
T	F	F	T	F	
F	T	T	F	T	Invalid
F	F	T	T	T	

Look to the column for the argument's conclusion (in this case, ~S) and check to see which of its rows have an F. Then check each of those rows to see if all the premises are true in that row. If there is any row in which all the premises are true and the conclusion is false, then the argument is invalid.

With this example, you see that the conclusion, ~S, is false in the first row and the third row. Looking at the first row, you see that one premise is false (~A) and the other premise is true (A → S). This means that this combination is okay—it doesn't show the argument is invalid. However, in the third row ~A is true and A → S is also true. This means that it is possible for all of the premises to be true and the conclusion to be false. Therefore, the argument is invalid.

Here is another example:

If it is Sunny, then Everyone will be happy. If Everyone is happy, then Michael will be happy. It is Sunny, therefore Michael will be happy.

The first two steps are to assign variable letters and translate the argument into variable and logical connectives, resulting in the following:

P1) S → E

P2) E → M

P3) S

_____

C4) ∴ M

Step 3: Create your top line. Since you have already listed M as a variable, you don't need to put the conclusion M down a second time.

| Premise 3 | | Conclusion 4 | Premise 1 | Premise 2 |
S	E	M	S→E	E→M

Step 4: Fill in the possible truth value combinations, beginning with the variables. Three terms equals eight possibilities:

| Premise 3 | | Conclusion 4 | Premise 1 | Premise 2 |
S	E	M	S→E	E→M
T	T	T		
T	T	F		
T	F	T		
T	F	F		
F	T	T		
F	T	F		
F	F	T		
F	F	F		

Now complete the truth table:

| Premise 3 | | Conclusion 4 | Premise 1 | Premise 2 |
S	E	M	S→E	E→M
T	T	T	T	T
T	T	F	T	F
T	F	T	F	T
T	F	F	F	T
F	T	T	T	T
F	T	F	T	F
F	F	T	T	T
F	F	F	T	T

Step 5: Find where the conclusion is false and check to see if all the premises along any of those rows are true. If in any row the premises are all true and the conclusion is false, then the argument is invalid.

The conclusion M is false in every second row. But whenever it is false, there is at least one false premise. Thus, the argument is valid.

Here is one more example, already symbolized.

P1) (S → C) v P
_____

C2) ∴ S v ~P

Notice in this example that you have two complex statements, meaning that you'll have to include component statements in the truth table. Remember that both bracketed statements and negated variables count as component statements and need their own columns. You'll need to figure out the truth values of ~P before you can figure out those of S v ~P; and you'll need to figure out the truth values of (S → C) before you can figure out those of (S → C) v P. First, let's fill in the top row with the variables, component statements, premises, and conclusion.

| | | | | | Premise 1 | Conclusion 2 |
S	C	P	~P	S→C	(S→C) v P	S v ~P

Now let's fill in the truth values for the variables and then the component statements:

| | | | | | Premise 1 | Conclusion 2 |
S	C	P	~P	S→C	(S→C) v P	S v ~P
T	T	T	F	T		
T	T	F	T	T		
T	F	T	F	F		
T	F	F	T	F		
F	T	T	F	T		
F	T	F	T	T		
F	F	T	F	T		
F	F	F	T	T		

You may be wondering how we fill in the truth values for the complex statements on the right—after all, we've only so far looked at the truth tables for the four basic connectives (~, &, v, and →). But every complex statement can be viewed as an application of one of those four connectives. All we need to do is treat the component statements as though they were variables. Take the first complex statement:

(S → C) v P

With a simple (non-complex) disjunction, we already know how to fill in the truth table—look to the truth value of the variable on the left of the disjunction, then look to the truth value of the variable on the right of the disjunction and fill in the table according to the disjunction truth table given earlier. In this case, we have a component statement (S → C) rather than a variable on the left of the disjunction. But we know the truth values for that component statement; in fact, we've already filled them in! So we can determine the truth values of the complex disjunction just as we did the truth values of the simple disjunction:

						Premise 1
P	**Q**	**P v Q**		**S → C**	**P**	**(S → C) v P**
T	T	T		T	T	T
T	F	T		T	F	T
F	T	T		F	T	T
F	F	F		F	F	F
				T	T	T
				T	F	T
				T	T	T
				T	F	T

As with the simple truth table, the disjunction is true in every case except when the truth values of the statements both to the left and to the right of the disjunction are false.

The truth values for the other complex statement in this argument, S v ~P, can be filled in using the same method, that is, by looking to the truth values of S and ~P and comparing them to our truth table for disjunction. As a result, we get the following:

					Premise 1	Conclusion 2	
S	**C**	**P**	**~P**	**S → C**	**(S → C) v P**	**S v ~P**	
T	T	T	F	T	T	T	
T	T	F	T	T	T	T	
T	F	T	F	F	T	T	
T	F	F	T	F	F	T	
F	T	T	F	T	T	F	Invalid
F	T	F	T	T	T	T	
F	F	T	F	T	T	F	Invalid
F	F	F	T	T	T	T	

Now we need only complete Step 5 to determine whether or not the argument is valid. Look to the conclusion first. Find when it is false. In this example it is false twice: the fourth last row and the second last row. Check along each row in which it is false to see if there is also at least one false premise (make sure you're looking only at complete premises, not at the components). If there is at least one false premise, then that combination is fine. In this example there is only one premise, and it is true in both rows where the conclusion is false. Therefore, the argument is invalid.

8.4 Creating Short Truth Tables

Since the fifth step of the long truth table method only requires that you examine the possible combinations when the conclusion is false, you can determine the validity of propositional arguments faster by not bothering to write down the other possible combinations. This is called the **short truth table method**. This method involves doing most of the calculations in your head instead of down on paper. That might sound scary, but if you look at any long truth table, you will notice that you often only require a fraction of its details to assess validity since you ignore all the work you did for the lines in which the conclusion is true or the premises false. Here are the steps of the short truth table method:

1. Determine the argument's variables; translate its statements into variables and logical connectives; and fill in the top row of a truth table with variables, component statements, premises, and the conclusion. This is the same as Steps 1 to 3 of the long truth table method, except that you can start out with only one row in your truth table.
2. *Assume the conclusion is false* (put F in the column for the conclusion). Then set the truth values of the variables and component statements that are included in the conclusion accordingly. (If the conclusion is S v P, for example, make both S and P false so that the whole disjunction is false.) If several different combinations of truth values would make the conclusion false, add additional rows to represent each combination. For example, if the conclusion is S & P, you'll need three rows to represent every combination in which S & P is false (S is true, P is false; S is false, P is true; S is false, P is false).
3. The truth values you have already filled in might dictate the truth values of other component statements and/or premises in the chart. If this is the case, fill those in. For example, if in Step 2 S and P were both assigned truth-values of F, then if S v P is one of the argument's premises or component statements, fill in its truth value as F (since it must be false if S and P are both false).
4. For each of the rows you have already created, *assume the premises are true* (i.e., see if you can put T in the columns for each of the premises). Then, see if you can fill in the truth values of the variables and component statements that make up those premises. If there is more than one way you can do this for a given row, you will need to add a row to the truth table to show each variation. If the truth values you

Short Truth Table Method: A technique used in propositional logic to determine an argument's validity. In this technique, one begins by assigning the truth value of the conclusion to false and then filling in a table so as to determine whether the premises can all be true while the conclusion is false. If they can, then the argument is invalid.

have determined so far affect the truth values of any other component statements or premises, try to fill in those truth values consistently. At any point in this process, you may discover a contradiction—you may end up needing to set the truth value of a variable or component statement to T when it has already been filled in as F (or vice versa) in Steps 2 or 3. If this happens, circle the contradictory truth value on that row to indicate that it is not a case in which the premises are true and the conclusion false; you are then done with that row.

5. Stop when either (a) you have completed a row in which the premises are true without finding any contradictions or (b) you have filled out a row for every possible set of truth values in which the premises are all true and the conclusion is false and you have found a contradiction in every one. If you stop at (a)—that is, if there is at least one row in which the premises are true, the conclusion is false, and there are no contradictions—then it is possible for the premises to be true and the conclusion false, so the argument is invalid. If you stop at (b)—that is, if every row either requires that a premise be false or includes a contradiction ~, then the argument is deductively valid.

Here's one of the examples that we already calculated using the long truth table method; compare the answers if you'd like.

P1) S → E
P2) E → M
P3) S
_____
C4) ∴ M

Since the argument is already translated, we can go ahead and create a table to complete Step 1.

Premise 3		Conclusion 4	Premise 1	Premise 2
S	E	M	S → E	E → M

Now make the conclusion, M, false. Since that doesn't determine the truth value of any other columns, we can move directly to Step 4 and begin making the premises true.

Premise 3		Conclusion 4	Premise 1	Premise 2
S	E	M	S → E	E → M
T		F	T	T

If S is true, then for S → E to be true, E has to be true. If E is true, then E → M is false, since M is known to be false from Step 2. But we have already assumed

E → M to be true since it is a premise; so we've arrived at a contradiction. Circle that spot to indicate that a contradiction has been reached. This means that at least one of the premises has to be false in order for the conclusion to be false, and so the argument is valid.

Premise 3		Conclusion 4	Premise 1	Premise 2
S	E	M	S→E	E→M
T	T	F	T	(F)

Let's try another:

P1) A → S

P2) S → A

C3) ∴ A & S

Once you have created the top row of your table, begin by making the conclusion false. A conjunction can be false in any of three ways, so we'll need to add extra rows to the truth table to represent each possibility. Remember to fill in the values that have already been determined (in this case, the F for A & S) on every row.

		Premise 1	Premise 2	Conclusion 3
A	S	A→S	S→A	A & S
T	F			F
F	T			F
F	F			F

Now move on to Step 3. Since each of the variables has already been assigned a truth value, we can fill in the truth values for each of the remaining statements, just as we would using the long truth table method.

		Premise 1	Premise 2	Conclusion 3
A	S	A→S	S→A	A & S
T	F	F	T	F
F	T	T	F	F
F	F	T	T	F

That's it for Step 3. Step 4 requires that we assume the premises are true; on the first two rows, this leads to some contradictions, so we'll circle the contradictory truth-values.

		Premise 1	Premise 2	Conclusion 3	
A	S	A→S	S→A	A & S	
T	F	(F)	T	F	
F	T	T	(F)	F	
F	F	T	T	F	Invalid

One row of the truth table did not lead to a contradiction and has both true premises and a false conclusion. Therefore, it is possible to make both premises true while the conclusion is false. So the argument is invalid.

Note that if you have to insert additional rows in order to represent different possible truth value combinations, then you won't know that the argument is valid until you've checked each and every row. However, if you find any row in which the premises are true and the conclusion is false (without a contradiction), then the argument is invalid.

One last one for you. Before you read the explanation, try to fill out the short truth table for this question on your own.

P1) $(S \to C) \lor P$

_____

C2) $\therefore S \lor \sim P$

First, make the conclusion false; then make S false and $\sim P$ false (this is the only way the conclusion could be false). If $\sim P$ is false, then P must be true. But then, no matter what C is, the premise will turn out to be true, since at least one half of the disjunction is true already. We've now filled in the truth value for the argument's only premise and can therefore skip Step 4, even though some parts of the truth tree haven't been filled in. Since it's possible for the conclusion to be false and the premise true, the argument is invalid. Here's the completed table:

				Premise 1	Conclusion 2		
S	C	P	~P	(S→C) v P	S v ~P	S→C	
F		T	F	T	F		Invalid

Remember that the short truth table method is just a faster version of the long truth table method. So if you find the short truth table method difficult, you can always construct a long truth table instead, as they are equally effective at demonstrating validity and invalidity.

8.5 Chapter Exercises

Exercise 8.1

TRUE/FALSE QUESTIONS

1. "Pauline can Buy a new car only if she Sells her old one" can be accurately formalized as B → S. True or False?
2. "Neither Brea nor Travis will pass their driver's test" can be accurately formalized as ~B v ~T. True or False?
3. If "Hitler died in 1945" is P, then ~P is "It is not the case that Hitler died in 1945." True or False?

4. In a long truth table you need a column representing each statement. True or False?
5. If P is false and Q is true, then P v Q is true and Q → P is true. True or False?

Exercise 8.2

Translate the following into propositional logic.

1. If the children are ill and the babysitter is too, then either Mom or Dad will have to stay home.
2. Having insurance is important for business owners unless they want to risk losing everything.
3. It's not the case that if people were angels, then there would be no need for the Rule of Law.
4. Plato's *Republic* is a great work, but it's not an easy text to read.
5. If the ceasefire holds, then we will see peace and stability return to the region.
6. Either Paul or Quinton won an award, if Rachel won.
7. Either Francine or Jenna will make the lacrosse team, but not both of them. If Francine does, she will be happy. If Jenna does, she'll be playing both lacrosse and soccer this season.
8. If dinner is ready on time and the traffic is light, we should make it to the theatre before the curtain rises. Dinner was not ready on time although the traffic was light. We did not make it to the theatre in time for the curtain.
9. If the ticket office is open but you buy your ticket on the ferry, you will be charged an additional $10.00.
10. In order to pass the course, one only needs to get a grade of B or C.

Exercise 8.3

Use the long truth table method to determine the validity or invalidity of the following arguments:

1. P1) A & B
   _____
   C2) ∴ (A & B) & (B & A)

2. P1) A & ~B
   _____
   C2) ∴ (A → B) & (B → A)

3. P1) A v B
   P2) C
   _____
   C3) ∴ (A → B) v (A & B)

4. P1) A
   P2) ~B
   _____
   C3) ∴ (A & B) v (A & B)

5. P1) A
   _____
   C2) ∴ (A & B) → A

Exercise 8.4

Use the short truth table method to determine the validity or invalidity of the following arguments:

1. P1) P
   P2) ~Q
   _____
   C3) ∴ ~(P v Q)

2. P1) P & ~Q
   _____
   C2) ∴ ~P → Q

3. P1) P
   _____
   C2) ∴ ~(P & ~Q)

4. P1) P → Q
   _____
   C2) ∴ ~(P → ~Q)

5. P1) P v ~Q
   P2) R
   _____
   C3) ∴ P & Q

Exercise 8.5

Use either the long or the short truth table method to determine the validity or invalidity of the following arguments:

1. P1) S → (M & P)
   P2) S v ~S
   P3) ~M → P
   _____
   C4) ∴ ~S

2. P1) P → ~Q
   P2) P & Q
   _____
   C3) ∴ Q

3. P1) $(A \& B) \to C$

    P2) $\sim C$

    _____

    C3) $\therefore \sim A \lor \sim B$

4. P1) $P \to (Q \lor P)$

    P2) $\sim Q \lor P$

    _____

    C3) $\therefore P \to Q$

5. P1) $P \lor (Q \& T)$

    P2) $\sim P \to T$

    P3) $T \to \sim Q$

    _____

    C4) $\therefore P \lor Q$

Exercise 8.6

1. Get used to "reading" propositional logic. Create a string of sentences using only variables and connectives. Then, exchange your string with a colleague and try reading your colleague's string out loud. For example, "$(P \lor Q) \to \sim F$" becomes (when read out loud) "If P or Q, then not F."

2. Next, create two or three ordinary English propositions and then transpose those into the variables of your string of propositional logic sentences. These do not have to make sense; they're just for practice, to get you comfortable reading symbols. For example, say that P is "Plants are green," Q is "I quit work before 5 p.m.," F is "Friends make life interesting." Now, when read out loud, "$(P \lor Q) \to \sim F$" becomes the rather strange sentence "If plants are green or I quit work before 5 p.m., then friends do not make life interesting."

8.6 Postscript

In this chapter, you have been introduced to propositional logic, the most basic system of what is called "symbolic logic." Since it looks a bit like math, this logic may have either scared you or made you feel more comfortable. Here, you saw more examples of logical patterns of reasoning and the means to establish conclusions with deductive certainty. Long truth tables allow you to systematically determine whether a deductive argument is valid. Short truth tables take a bit more getting used to, but with practice they can become a quicker and more efficient method of determining validity.

Be sure that you try to make up propositional arguments on your own. They don't have to be difficult or complicated, and they don't have to be valid. Start with simple ones so that you begin to recognize their different logical patterns, and don't get overwhelmed by complex arguments—simply break them down into their smallest parts and apply the truth table methods. Practice makes perfect!

And so here we are! Finished! You have explored numerous elements that will help you in your everyday life as well as your academic and professional one. This is because you have had the opportunity to sharpen your reasoning skills to the point where anything you think about from now on will be done within the context of understanding and appreciating the art and science (not to mention the challenges) of critical thinking.

Solutions to Chapter Exercises

Chapter 1

Exercise 1.1

1. False. The sentence is simply an unsupported claim.
2. True. This is the role of premises.
3. True. This is basically a definition of an argument.
4. False. The premises might be about some subject other than the conclusion, or they might offer only inadequate support for the conclusion.
5. True. That statement is used to support the claim that the library is a useful place.

Exercise 1.2

1. Just a description.
2. An explanation.
3. A description of a certain state of affairs. This passage could also be interpreted as an argument, with the first sentence as the conclusion and the last three sentences as premises.
4. A set of historical facts.
5. A description.
6. An argument. There are actually two conclusions here. (1) The lawyers think the person would be fair. (2) The person will be chosen to be on the jury. The first conclusion is used as a premise alongside the earlier claim about how lawyers pick jury members to support the second conclusion that the individual will be chosen for the jury. Remember to ask yourself, "What is the main idea here?" Notice that the use of the indicator phrase "this is good enough evidence to conclude that" tells us where both the premise and conclusion are. As well, there is the conclusion indicator "Accordingly." Again, these details are things you will learn in this text.
7. An argument. The person is using the first two statements to convince us that the term "global warming" is not correct—that more things are going on besides just "warming." Note the use of the premise and conclusion indicator "these events tell us." It is a premise indicator because "these events" refer to the passage's premises/reasons; it is indicating the conclusion by the use of "tell us."
8. An argument. Pay attention to the fact that the conclusion is actually the second sentence: Athletes will try anything, including cheating, to win.
9. An argument. Here there is one long (and run on) sentence that forms an entire argument. The conclusion is the first thing stated: If you are planning on visiting Europe this summer, it is a good idea to learn a few basic foreign words and expressions. This is followed by a premise indicator "because." The word "so" is not being used as a conclusion indicator here. There are two premises: "there are so many opportunities to travel" and "if you are lost, you increase your chances of getting help by being able to communicate."

Exercise 1.5

1. (a) The speaker's conclusion is the first statement. The judgement is not that the speaker should take philosophy or how bad he or she will be at it. Rather, regardless of the merits of taking philosophy, the speaker believes there are many reasons not to enroll in the course.
2. (a) BP's problems are given as an example of one of the many problems that support the condemnation of offshore drilling. The main idea is that such practices should be stopped.
3. (c) There are many goalies and many teams in need of goalies, so the person concludes that many goalies will be chosen early.
4. (b) There are thinkers on campus with new ideas that may be considered radical.
5. (b) The person is talking about the role of violence and argues that television shows set in Ancient Greece or medieval Europe would not be good shows without violence. Like all of the arguments presented, whether the claims made are actually good is not the point. Rather, the important thing here is that the person has offered an argument with premises and a conclusion and that you are able to distinguish between them.
6. Typical examples: because, since, due to.
7. Typical examples: accordingly, it follows that, therefore.
8. For example: Given that apples are good for you and since oranges provide vitamin C, fruits should be eaten daily.
9. For example: NASA has images of Saturn that show it to be a dead planet. There is no life on Saturn.
10. The word "argument" should only have one "e." This is a very common spelling error that you should avoid!

Chapter 2

Exercise 2.1

1. True.
2. False. As discussed in Chapter 1, violent disagreements are not arguments. So this definition is not too narrow, it is simply incorrect.
3. True. In the first case, "same" means "exactly alike"; in the second case, "same" means "similar in relevant respects."
4. False. In some contexts, when you are not making an argument but rather conveying your feelings, emotionally charged language is appropriate.
5. False. The passage relies on a very strange definition of "free," but its meaning is clear.

Exercise 2.2

1. Many other things are toys for children but not dolls, such as toy cars, Slinkies, etc. Also, some dolls are not intended for children, namely, expensive collectible dolls. So the definition is too broad AND too narrow.
2. You would not refer to a female dog as a "woman," nor would you call a young girl a woman. Only an adult female human counts as a woman. The definition is too broad.
3. This is too narrow a definition, as gloves are also used for cycling, fashion, and other purposes. It is also too broad a definition, as it would seem to include mittens.
4. "Fairness" is vague. The definition doesn't seem to tell us any more than did the original term.
5. a. While you can easily point to a friend, it would be difficult for another person to understand what exactly it is about him or her that you are trying to identify (clothes, hair, gender, height, age, etc.). So an ostensive definition would be difficult.
   b. You can fake a sneeze and that counts as an ostensive definition. In fact, trying to provide a stipulative definition for "sneeze" would be pretty hard! Try it!

c. For "cold," you could just hand the person an ice cube and some other cold objects to provide an ostensive definition

d. You may show different forms of entertainment, but the term applies to so many pleasant diversions that it may just be clearer to offer a reportive definition.

e. Although you cannot point to a dream, and so can't provide an ostensive definition (if by "dream" you mean a series of visual experiences and sensations that you have while sleeping), you can probably offer a reasonably good description of one.

f. If by "bright" you mean a bright light, you might provide an ostensive definition by simply pointing to a bright light bulb. If by "bright" you mean someone of high intelligence (e.g., "she is bright for her age"), an ostensive definition would probably be difficult.

Exercise 2.7

1. A C D B
2. D C B A
3. B D A C
4. C A D B

Chapter 3

Exercise 3.1

1. False. The argument might be weakened, but it would still make logical sense.
2. True. The scope "Many" is narrower than "All."
3. True. The intermediate conclusion of the sub-argument is "Jim probably won't leave his apartment today."
4. True. The arguer is assuming incorrectly that anything natural will be safe.
5. False. The missing conclusion is that the walls are too thin.

Exercise 3.4

1. Missing conclusion: It is hot.

   P1) I will burn my tongue if it is hot.
   P2) I burnt my tongue.
   _____
   MC3) Therefore, it is hot.

2. Missing premise: It will rain and I will get wet.
   Missing premise: If it rains and I get wet, when I get home tonight I will have to change out of my soaked clothes.

   P1) Either it will be sunny today or it will rain and I will get wet.
   MP2) It will rain and I will get wet.
   MP3) If it rains and I get wet, when I get home tonight I will have to change out of my soaked clothes.
   _____
   C4) Therefore, when I get home tonight I will have to change out of my soaked clothes.

3. Missing conclusion: This polar bear is wearing a toque.

   P1) All polar bears wear toques.
   P2) Here's a polar bear.
   _____
   MC3) Therefore, this polar bear is wearing a toque.

4. Missing conclusion: It is not a spider over there.

   P1) If it is a spider over there, then you will hear me scream in a minute.
   P2) I didn't scream.
   _____
   MC3) Therefore, it is not a spider over there.

Exercise 3.5

1. Independent

   P1) The weather was fine.

   P2) The people were friendly,

   P3) The music was nice

   P4) The food was great.

   C5) Therefore, all in all, it was a good day.

2. Independent

   P1) You stumble when you walk.

   P2) You mumble instead of talking.

   P3) You seem not to notice that your right arm is at an unnatural angle.

   P4) You are apparently attracted to my brain and not my beauty.

   C5) Therefore, you must be a zombie.

3. Dependent

   P1) If they don't finish the voting recount soon, we won't know who won until tomorrow.

   P2) They are finished counting the votes.

   MC3) Therefore, we don't have to wait until tomorrow to find out who won.

4. Dependent

   P1) We will only know if you are allergic to the food after you eat it.

   P2) You only had one bite and now you're covered in hives.

   MP3) If you get hives after eating something, you must be allergic to it.

   C4) Therefore, I guess you must be allergic to the food!

5. Independent

   P1) The tax increase will help offset any environmental costs.

   P2) The tax increase will help fix the bridges.

   P3) The tax increase will provide the government officials with a nice pension.

   C4) Therefore, the tax increase will be beneficial for a variety of reasons.

Chapter 4

Exercise 4.1

1. False. An argument may have satisfactory and supportive premises that fail to offer *sufficient* support for the conclusion.
2. False. The premise gives some support but not enough. Perhaps I was forced to take the dog for some reason.
3. False. Sometimes we cannot obtain certainty about a premise but it is still reasonable to believe, for example, "The sun will rise tomorrow."
4. False. Statements are true or false, not whole arguments. Arguments can be successful or unsuccessful.
5. False. The premise that is missing may be logically required. In such cases, it is your job to insert any missing premises.

Exercise 4.4

1. A does not support B.
2. A does not support B. A is obviously false, but even if it were true, it wouldn't support B.
3. A supports B.
4. A most likely supports B, but only if we add the missing premise that "The defence wants an honest and reliable witness."
5. A supports B.
6. A supports B with the missing premise that "Skating skills and hand-eye coordination are required to move a puck around the ice."
7. A does not support B.
8. A does not support B.
9. A does not support B. In fact, it is negatively relevant to B.
10. A does not support B.

Exercise 4.5

1. Satisfactory: Common knowledge
2. Unsatisfactory: Improper appeal to expert authority since this view is not shared by most other scientists (and your friend may or may not be an authority in the relevant scientific discipline).
3. Unsatisfactory: Appeals to personal testimony but goes beyond that testimony to make a general conclusion based on an inadequate sample.
4. Unsatisfactory: Vague. How big is "big" or "huge"?
5. Unsatisfactory: Refutable by common knowledge.
6. Unsatisfactory: Ambiguous. Is the statement about Victor's emotional state or his colour?
7. Satisfactory: Personal Testimony.

Exercise 4.6

1. P1) Birds can fly.
   P2) Bats can fly.
   P3) I can fly.
   _____
   C4) Therefore, all living things can fly.

   Step 1, Satisfactoriness: P1 needs to be clarified, as the statement is ambiguous. Does it mean "all birds" or "some birds"; some birds, such as penguins and ostriches, cannot fly. P2 has the same ambiguity (does it mean "all bats" or "some bats"), but either interpretation would be satisfactory because it is common knowledge that (all) bats can fly. P3 is ambiguous—surely people cannot fly without some sort of mechanical assistance, but they can fly in airplanes. So either P3 means that "I can fly in an airplane," in which case it's common knowledge and therefore satisfactory, or it means that "I can fly without assistance," in which case it's unsatisfactory.

   Step 2, Support: The conclusion is similarly ambiguous, and so it is difficult to assess whether P3 offers any support.

   Step 3, Sufficient Support: Even if we ignore the ambiguities in the premises and conclusion, when we move to the third step of the S-Test we can see that the argument clearly fails, as its premises do not offer *sufficient* support for its very broad conclusion. This is an inductive argument.

2. P1) All mammals have DNA.
    P2) I am a mammal.
    _____
    C3) Therefore, I have DNA.

    Step 1, Satisfactoriness: P1 is common knowledge and therefore satisfactory. P2 is personal testimony and obviously true (since all humans are mammals).

    Step 2, Support: Taken together as dependent premises, these premises offer some support for the conclusion.

    Step 3, Sufficient Support: This is a deductive argument. The conclusion cannot be false if the premises are true, so the premises do indeed offer sufficient support for the conclusion. This is therefore a successful argument.

3. P1) Everyday around noon, my boss has ordered the same thing for lunch.
    P2) My boss always calls me to place the order for him.
    P3) It is almost noon now.
    _____
    C4) Therefore, he will soon be calling me to place an order for his usual lunch.

    Step 1, Satisfactoriness: P1 is satisfactory as it is personal testimony. Assuming the speaker is honest and reliable, there is no reason to doubt the claim. This also applies for P2. P3 can be confirmed by looking at a clock (or a couple of clocks).

    Step 2, Support: The premises support the conclusion, as in combination they are all relevant to it.

    Step 3, Sufficient Support: The conclusion seems highly likely, given the premises; that is, the premises do indeed offer sufficient support. Although the conclusion is not guaranteed, the argument passes the S-Test and thus is successful. This is an inductive argument.

4. P1) Jazz is made up of complex arrangements, like classical music.
    P2) Classical music has been around for centuries and has withstood the passage of time.
    _____
    C3) Therefore, I suspect jazz will also be around for centuries and withstand the passage of time.

    Note that the first sentence in this passage begins with the conclusion of the argument, so you need to be careful in standardizing the argument correctly. Note that it is an argument from analogy since it is comparing Jazz and Classical music.

    Step 1, Satisfactoriness: P1 is satisfactory; it may be common knowledge, but if you were uncertain about it, you could do some research or consult appropriate authorities. P2 is also satisfactory, since it is common knowledge that the classical genre is still around.

    Step 2, Support: Because the premises point out a similarity between classical music and jazz, they offer some support to the conclusion, which suggests that jazz will resemble classical music in another respect.

    Step 3, Sufficient Support: This argument doesn't point out enough similarities between classical music and jazz to show that jazz will "withstand the passage of time" in the same way as classical music. And so the argument fails the test for sufficiency.

5. P1) I have 2,000 comic books in my basement.
    P2) I have 4,000 more comics in my study.
    P3) I have 50 comics locked away in my safe.
    _____
    C4) Therefore, I have 6,050 comic books in total.

    Step 1, Satisfactoriness: In this argument P1, P2, and P3 are all satisfactory, as they are examples of personal testimony and there is no evidence to cast doubt on the honesty or reliability of the speaker.

Step 2, Support: Each premise is clearly relevant to the conclusion as they talk about numbers of comic books. So the premises pass the support test.

Step 3, Sufficient Support: Since the sums add up to 6,050, the conclusion is guaranteed by the premises. It would be impossible for the conclusion to be false and the premises true, so its premises thus sufficiently support its conclusion. It therefore passes the S-Test and is a successful argument.

6. P1) The weather along the east coast has been much more dramatic these past years.

   P2) Every year there have been more storms than the year before.

   P3) The storms have been stronger than ever.

   P4) It is almost winter.

   _____

   C5) Therefore, the people living along the East Coast should expect there to be some strong snowstorms, over and above what they have experienced in the last few years.

Step 1, Satisfactoriness: The meteorologist is an acceptable authority concerning the satisfactoriness of premises 1, 2, and 3. P4 may or may not be true, depending on the time of year, but we can suppose here that the argument is being offered in late Fall and there's no reason to doubt the claim, so this premise can be considered common knowledge.

Step 2, Support: Each of the first three premises, when combined with P4, inductively supports the conclusion.

Step 3, Sufficient Support: Given that the conclusion uses the expression "should expect," it has been qualified and does not claim that significant weather events are guaranteed. As such, the premises offer sufficient support for the conclusion; thus, this is a successful argument.

7. P1) Most people need regular exercise to stay healthy as they get older.

   P2) You're no longer young.

   _____

   MC3) Therefore, you need regular exercise to stay healthy.

   P4) Cycling is a great way to exercise.

   _____

   C5) Therefore, you should try cycling if you want to stay healthy.

This argument leaves out the implied statement linking cycling with its main conclusion. The missing conclusion comes out of a sub-argument established by the first two statements.

Step 1, Satisfactoriness: P1 is presumably common knowledge, but if uncertain you might ask some physicians to confirm this premise through expert authority. For the sake of this example, we'll assume P2 is true. P4 is also common knowledge.

Step 2, Support: P1 and P2 are dependent premises that work together to support the conclusion of the sub-argument, MC3. Likewise, MC3 and P4 work together to support the main conclusion, C5.

Step 3, Sufficient Support: The first premise is not a universal statement; its scope addresses the needs of "most" people but not all. So though MC3 is likely, it's not guaranteed; a better argument might limit the scope of MC3: "You *probably* need regular exercise to stay healthy." Nonetheless, since P1 covers most cases, it offers a fairly high degree of support in the sub-argument. Similarly, MC3 and P4 offer a reasonable degree of support for C5, but don't guarantee its truth (C5 could still be false if, for example, you have a medical condition that makes cycling difficult).

This is an example of an argument in which the conclusion is shown to be likely but is not guaranteed. We'll look more closely at arguments of this sort in the next chapter. In a case like this, we might say that the argument passes the S-Test, but that its conclusion is nonetheless uncertain.

8. P1) You committed stupid actions.

   MP2) Those who commit stupid actions have brains the size of dinosaur brains.

   ───────────

   C3) Therefore, your brain is about the size of a dinosaur's brain.

   P4) Dinosaurs didn't manage to live very long.

   ───────────

   MC5) Therefore, you will not live very long.

   ───────────

   C6) Therefore, I think you'd better smarten up.

   The first sentence is actually an argument on its own. The person making the argument infers a conclusion (about the size of "your" brain) on the basis of a premise (that "you" committed dumb actions). To connect P1 and C3, we need to add the missing premise MP2.

   Step 1, Satisfactoriness: There is no indication of what the arguer means by "dumb" and no examples are provided to illustrate the claim, so P1 is vague and therefore unsatisfactory. P1 might be satisfactory if its meaning was clarified, but only if the arguer's personal testimony is reliable (which, as the emotionally charged language suggests, it may not be) or we have other evidence demonstrating "your" dumb actions. MP2 is also unsatisfactory, and likely false, as science has shown that intelligence doesn't correlate with brain size.

   As discussed in Chapter 3, we can continue assessing a complex argument even if its sub-argument fails. To do so, we treat the conclusion of the sub-argument as a premise and ask whether it is satisfactory on its own; if it is, then it may still (along with any other remaining premises) offer sufficient support to the main conclusion, in which case the whole argument may succeed.

   However, the intermediate conclusion C3 isn't satisfactory on its own either and would require further evidence. P4 is ambiguous, since it could be a claim that dinosaurs as a group didn't live very long or a claim that individual dinosaurs didn't live very long. So it's unsatisfactory, but even if its meaning was clarified, it would still be unsatisfactory: it's common knowledge that dinosaurs as a group lived for millions of years, and a little research will tell you that experts believe some individual dinosaurs could live for very long indeed. Because C3 and P4 are not satisfactory, the second sub-argument also fails.

   Step 2, Support: C3 and P4 also fail to provide support for MC5. Even if they were both satisfactory, they wouldn't offer support unless some *further* missing premise, connecting brain size with longevity, were added.

   Step 3, Sufficient Support: As C3 and P4 don't provide any support for MC5, they certainly don't provide sufficient support. The second sub-argument therefore fails in all three respects: the premises are unsatisfactory and they don't provide sufficient support for MC5.

   Bypassing for now the question of whether MC5 is independently satisfactory, we can see that it would fail to sufficiently support C6 regardless, as it's not made clear how one's imminent death would be prevented by "smartening up." And so, the main argument, like the sub-arguments, fails.

9. P1) I have a bag of different coloured marbles.

   P2) Ten are black and two are red.

   P3) With my eyes closed, I just removed a red marble from the bag.

   ───────────

   C4) Therefore, the next one I remove will probably be black.

   Step 1, Satisfactoriness: P1, P2, and P3 are instances of personal testimony; let's assume here that the speaker is honest and reliable, and so the premises are satisfactory.

   Step 2, Support: The premises, when combined, support the conclusion.

   Step 3, Sufficient Support: Although the odds favour a black marble being selected next, there is a possibility that the speaker could remove the other red marble, so the premises don't definitively show that the next marble will be black. The conclusion, however, is qualified, not certain, and these premises are sufficient to support the conclusion that the next marble will *probably* be black. It's a successful argument.

Chapter 5

Exercise 5.1

1. False. Validity is a weaker requirement than soundness and only looks at the structure of the argument, not the truth value of the statements.
2. If an argument is sound, it must be valid. And if it is sound, it is a successful argument.
3. False. There may be dissimilarities but they will be irrelevant.
4. True. This is one of the functions of induction.
5. True. Inductive arguments deal with probabilities, not certainties and thus cannot guarantee the truth of the conclusion.

Exercise 5.2

1. Inductive.
2. Analogy.
3. Inductive.
4. Inductive.
5. Inductive.
6. Deductive.
7. Analogy.
8. Inductive.
9. Analogy.
10. Deductive.

Exercise 5.3

1. Inductive.
2. Deductive.
3. Analogy.

Exercise 5.6

1. This is a deductive argument. It is valid but not sound; it fails Step 1 of the S-Test but passes the other two steps.

    Step 1, Satisfactoriness: The second premise is satisfactory, as there is good reason to believe it is true; it's common knowledge that deadly nightshade is a plant, but if you weren't sure of this, it could easily be confirmed by consulting a relevant authority. The first premise, however, is not satisfactory—it is common knowledge that not everything that grows naturally is safe to eat. This means that the argument fails the S- Test, and it cannot be sound.

    Step 2, Support: Taken together as dependent premises, these premises offer support for the conclusion, so the argument passes this step of the S-Test.

    Step 3, Sufficient Support: Because this is a deductive argument, in order to pass this step of the S-Test, the argument must be valid—it must be impossible for the premises to be true and the conclusion to be false. If these premises were true, the conclusion would necessarily be true also, so the argument is valid and passes this step of the test.

2. This is an argument by analogy. It is strong; it passes all three steps of the S-Test.

    Step 1, Satisfactoriness: This is an inductive analogy, so we need to evaluate whether there is good reason to believe that each premise is true. The first premise is based on personal testimony, which we have no reason to disbelieve; it is therefore satisfactory. The second premise is also satisfactory—if it's not part of your general knowledge, it could easily be confirmed through research. The argument passes this step of the S-Test.

    Step 2, Support: Since the content of the book and of the movie are relevant to how scary each is, both premises are relevant to the conclusion. The argument therefore passes this step of the S-Test.

    Step 3, Sufficient Support: There are some differences between the book and the movie— for example the book was published in 1988 and the movie came out in 1991; the movie takes about two hours to watch while the book may take much longer to read— but none of these differences are relevant to the conclusion. The medium is different, of course, but, unless you have some reason to think that the speaker is more frequently frightened by books than by movies, this difference is not relevant either. The argument therefore passes this step of the S-Test as well. Since it passes all three steps, it is a strong argument by analogy.

3. This is an inductive argument. It fails the last step of the S-Test and is therefore weak.

   Step 1, Satisfactoriness: Since the premise is personal testimony, and we have no reason to disbelieve it, it is satisfactory. The argument passes this step of the S-Test.

   Step 2, Support: Since the conclusion concerns how many Canadians like Beethoven, and the premise concerns how many of a specific group of Canadians like Beethoven, the premise offers some degree of support for the conclusion. The argument passes this step of the S-Test.

   Step 3, Sufficient Support: This is a very small sample from which to draw conclusions about the whole population of Canada. Even more importantly, since members of the Toronto Symphony Orchestra are probably much more likely to enjoy a classical composer than are members of the general population, this is not a representative sample. We can't draw conclusions about all Canadians from this sample, so this argument fails this step of the S-Test and is weak.

4. This is an argument by analogy. It fails the second step of the S-Test and is therefore faulty.

   Step 1, Satisfactoriness: We are safe to assume that the speaker likely knows the names and home provinces of his or her own friends, and this information could be confirmed with research (i.e., by asking Carrie and Candice), so these premises are satisfactory. The argument passes the first step of the S-Test.

   Step 2, Support: The given similarities between Carrie and Candice—the fact that they are from the same province and their names start with the same letter—are not at all relevant to how well either of them did on the French test, so they don't offer any support for the conclusion. So the argument fails this step of the S-Test, and is therefore a faulty analogy.

   Step 3, Sufficient Support: Since the premises offer no support for the conclusion, they certainly don't offer sufficient support. The argument also fails this step of the S-Test.

5. This is a deductive argument. It passes all three steps of the S-Test and is therefore sound.

   Step 1, Satisfactoriness: Since it is common knowledge that any given cactus must be either dead or alive, the first premise is satisfactory. Let's assume that the second premise is also satisfactory; it could be confirmed by the examination of the cactus. The argument passes this step of the S-Test.

   Step 2, Support: Taken together, these premises offer support for the conclusion; the argument passes this step of the S-Test.

   Step 3, Sufficient Support: It is impossible for these premises to be true and the conclusion false. The argument passes this step of the S-Test, and is therefore valid. Since it also passes the first step of the S-Test, it is also sound.

Chapter 6

Exercise 6.1

1. False. A fallacy is, by definition, an error in reasoning (although it could be an intentional error).
2. False. People can commit fallacies unintentionally (perhaps because they haven't read this book yet!).
3. True. Insulting someone is not appropriate. Insulting is different from stating that a person is wrong.
4. False. Emotional reactions are appropriate at some times, and getting people excited about their team is not fallacious if it's not part of an argument.
5. False. You should presume others to be rational so that you do not accidentally commit the straw person fallacy.

Exercise 6.3

1(D), 2(B), 3(C), 4(F), 5(A), 6(E)

Exercise 6.4

1. Begging the Question
2. Two Wrongs Make a Right
3. Appeal to Tradition
4. Post hoc
5. Appeal to Popularity

6. Circumstantial Ad Hominem
7. Abusive Ad Hominem
8. Appeal to Pity
9. Slippery Slope
10. Improper Appeal to Authority

Exercise 6.5

1. Appeal to Force
2. Equivocation
3. Not Fallacious
4. Circumstantial Ad Hominem
5. Affirming the Consequent
6. Two Wrongs Make a Right
7. Not Fallacious
8. Inconsistency
9. Guilt by Association
10. Slippery Slope
11. Not Fallacious
12. Begging the Question
13. Appeal to Popularity
14. Hasty Generalization
15. Appeal to Ignorance
16. Division Fallacy
17. Denying the Antecedent

18. Abusive Ad Hominem
19. Post Hoc
20. Amphiboly
21. Not Fallacious
22. Not Fallacious
23. Appeal to Pity
24. Straw Person Argument
25. Not Fallacious
26. Appeal to Tradition
27. Composition Fallacy
28. Ad Hominem Tu Quoque
29. False Dilemma
30. Not Fallacious
31. Not Fallacious
32. Red Herring
33. Faulty Analogy
34. Improper Appeal to Authority

Chapter 7

Exercise 7.1

1. True.
2. False. A is false and I is false, but O is unknown.
3. True.
4. True.
5. False. It must tell you something about *every* member of the category.

Exercise 7.2

1. Invalid. There is a negative premise but an affirmative conclusion.
2. Invalid. The terms are distributed in the conclusion but not in the premises.
3. Invalid. The middle term is not distributed in either premise.

P1) All V are C.
P2) Some C are not R.
_____
C3) Therefore, some V are not R.

4. Valid. Satisfies all five rules.

   P1) No C are F.
   P2) All D are F.
   _____
   Therefore, no C are D.

5. Invalid. The second premise is negative, but the conclusion is affirmative.

   P1) Some S are not C.
   P2) No C are F.
   _____
   C3) Therefore, all F are S.

Exercise 7.3

1. All D are I.
2. All H are F.
3. Therefore, some A are C (or some C are A).
4. Therefore, some D are not C.
5. Therefore, all A are C.

Exercise 7.6

1. P1) No M are P = E
   P2) All S are M = A
   _____
   C3) Therefore, no S are P = E

   There are many ways to replace the variables in each of these questions. Here's one possible answer:

   P1) No living things are electronic.
   P2) All sentient things are living things.
   _____
   C3) Therefore, no sentient things are electronic.

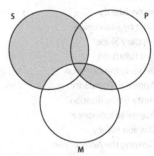

2. P1) No P are M = E
   P2) Some S are M = I
   _____
   C3) Therefore, some S are not P = O

   P1) No frogs are iguanas.
   P2) Some lizards are iguanas.
   _____
   C3) Therefore, some lizards are not frogs.

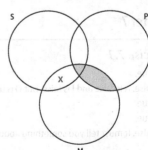

3. P1) Some M are not P = O
   P2) All M are S = A
   _____
   C3) Therefore, some S are not P = O

   P1) Some political debates are not interesting.
   P2) All political debates are important.
   _____
   C3) Therefore, some important things are
        not interesting.

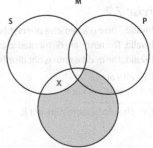

4. P1) All M are P = A
    P2) Some S are M = I

    C3) Therefore, some S are P = I

    P1) All tornadoes are dangerous.
    P2) Some natural disasters are tornadoes.

    C3) Therefore, some natural disasters are dangerous.

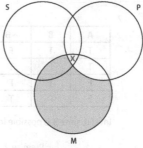

5. P1) All M are P = A
    P2) All S are M = A

    C3) Therefore, all S are P = A

    P1) All poodles are dogs.
    P2) All dogs are mammals.

    C3) Therefore, all poodles are mammals.

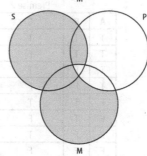

Chapter 8

Exercise 8.1

1. True.
2. False; the correct formalization is ~B & ~T.
3. True.
4. True.
5. False; P v Q is true, but P → Q is false.

Exercise 8.2

1. (C & B) → (M v D)
2. ~R → I
3. ~(A → ~R)
4. R & ~T
5. C → (P & S)
6. R → (P v Q)
7. (F v J) & ~ (F & J); F → H; J → (L & S)
8. (D & L) → T; ~D & L; ∴ ~T (note that this is *not* a valid argument)
9. (O & B) → A
10. (B v C) → P

Exercise 8.3

1.

		Premise 1		Conclusion 2
A	**B**	**A & B**	**B & A**	**(A & B) & (B & A)**
T	T	T	T	T
T	F	F	F	F
F	T	F	F	F
F	F	F	F	F

Valid, since the conclusion is only false when at least one of the premises is also false.

2.

					Premise 1	Conclusion 2
A	B	~B	A → B	B → A	A & ~B	(A → B) & (B → A)
T	T	F	T	T	F	T
T	F	T	F	T	T	F
F	T	F	T	F	F	F
F	F	T	T	T	F	T

Inv.

Invalid, since it is possible for the conclusion to be false and the premises true.

3.

		Premise 2			Premise 1	Conclusion 3
A	B	C	A → B	A & B	A v B	(A → B) v (A & B)
T	T	T	T	T	T	T
T	T	F	T	T	T	T
T	F	T	F	F	T	F
T	F	F	F	F	T	F
F	T	T	T	F	T	T
F	T	F	T	F	T	T
F	F	T	T	F	F	T
F	F	F	T	F	F	T

Invalid

Invalid, since it is possible for the conclusion to be false and the premises true.

4.

Premise 1		Premise 2		Conclusion 3
A	B	~B	A & B .	(A & B) v (A & B)
T	T	F	T	T
T	F	T	F	F
F	T	F	F	F
F	F	T	F	F

Invalid

Invalid, since it is possible for the conclusion to be false and the premises true.

5.

Premise 1			Conclusion 2
A	B	A & B	(A & B) → A
T	T	T	T
T	F	F	T
F	T	F	T
F	F	F	T

Valid, since the conclusion is never false.

Exercise 8.4

(Note that there are other possible ways of filling out the short truth tables.)

1.

Premise 1	Premise 2			Conclusion 3
P	Q	~Q	P v Q	~(P v Q)
T	T	F	T	F
T	F	T	T	F
F	T	F	T	F

Invalid, since it is possible for the conclusion to be false and the premises true.

2.

				Premise 1	Conclusion 2
P	Q	~P	~Q	P & ~Q	~P → Q
F	F	T	T	(F)	F

Valid, since the conclusion is only false when at least one of the premises is also false.

3.   Premise 1   Conclusion 2

			Premise 1	Conclusion 2	
P	Q	~Q	P & ~Q	~(P & ~Q)	
T	F	T	T	F	Invalid

Invalid, since it is possible for the conclusion to be false and the premises true.

4.

				Premise 1	Conclusion 2	
P	Q	~Q	P → ~Q	P → Q	~(P → ~Q)	
T	F	T	T	(F)	F	
F	F	T	T	T	F	Invalid
F	T	F	T	T	F	Invalid

Invalid, since it is possible for the conclusion to be false and the premises true.

5.

		Premise 2		Premise 1	Conclusion 3	
P	Q	R	~Q	P v ~Q	P & Q	
T	F	T	T	T	F	Invalid
F	T	T	F	(F)	F	
F	F	T	T	T	F	Invalid

Invalid, since it is possible for the conclusion to be false and the premises true.

Exercise 8.5

(Only the long truth table method is shown.)

1.

			Conclusion 4			Premise 2	Premise 3	Premise 1	
S	M	P	~S	~M	M & P	S v ~S	~M → P	S → (M & P)	
T	T	T	F	F	T	T	T	T	Invalid
T	T	F	F	F	F	T	T	F	
T	F	T	F	T	F	T	T	F	
T	F	F	F	T	F	T	F	F	
F	T	T	T	F	T	T	T	T	
F	T	F	T	F	F	T	T	T	
F	F	T	T	F	F	T	T	T	
F	F	F	T	T	F	T	F	T	

Invalid, since the premises are all true when the conclusion is false in the first row.

2.

			Conclusion 3	Premise 1	Premise 2
P	Q	~Q	P→~Q	P&Q
T	T	F	F	T
T	F	T	T	F
F	T	F	T	F
F	F	T	T	F

Valid, since the conclusion is only false when at least one of the premises is also false.

3.

					Premise 2		Premise 1	Conclusion 3
A	B	C	~A	~B	~C	A & B	(A & B)→C	~Av~B
T	T	T	F	F	F	T	T	F
T	T	F	F	F	T	T	F	F
T	F	T	F	T	F	F	T	T
T	F	F	F	T	T	F	T	T
F	T	T	T	F	F	F	T	T
F	T	F	T	F	T	F	T	T
F	F	T	T	T	F	F	T	T
F	F	F	T	T	T	F	T	T

Valid, since the conclusion is only false when at least one of the premises is also false.

4.

				Premise 1	Premise 2	Conclusion 3	
P	Q	~Q	QvP	P→(QvP)	~QvP	P→Q	
T	T	F	T	T	T	T	
T	F	T	T	T	T	F	Invalid
F	T	F	T	T	F	T	
F	F	T	F	T	T	T	

Invalid, since it is possible for the conclusion to be false and the premises true.

5.

						Premise 1	Premise 2	Premise 3	Conclusic
P	Q	T	~P	~Q	Q&T	Pv(Q&T)	~P→T	T→~Q	PvQ
T	T	T	F	F	T	T	T	F	T
T	T	F	F	F	F	F	T	T	T
T	F	T	F	T	F	F	T	T	T
T	F	F	F	T	F	F	T	T	T
F	T	T	T	F	T	T	T	F	T
F	T	F	T	F	F	F	F	T	T
F	F	T	T	T	F	F	T	T	F
F	F	F	T	T	F	F	F	T	F

Valid, since the conclusion is only false when at least one of the premises is also false.

Glossary of Key Terms

A priori **Analogy**: An argument by analogy in which the analogue case can be hypothetical or fictitious because the relevant similarities between the analogue and the primary subject don't depend on the existence of the analogue. (*Chapter 5*)

A Statement: A categorical statement of the form "All S are P." This states that all members of S are members of P. Also called a "universal affirmative." (*Chapter 7*)

Abusive Ad Hominem (Fallacy): A fallacy in which an individual's character is attacked, rather than his or her arguments. (*Chapter 6*)

Ad Hominem Tu Quoque (Fallacy): A fallacy in which an argument is rejected because the arguer does not act in accordance with his or her own conclusion. In Latin, *tu quoque* means "you too." (*Chapter 6*)

Affirming the Consequent (Fallacy): Any argument of the following form: If A, then B. B. Therefore, A. This argument form is always invalid. (*Chapter 6*)

Ambiguity: When a word or sentence has more than one possible meaning. (*Chapter 2*)

Amphiboly (Fallacy): A fallacy in which the structure of a sentence allows two different interpretations. (*Chapter 6*)

Analogue: What the primary subject is being compared to in an argument from analogy. (*Chapter 5*)

Antecedent: The first proposition in an "If ..., then ..." statement (a conditional statement), immediately following the "If." In the conditional statement "If P, then Q," P is the antecedent. (*Chapter 8*)

Appeal to Force (Fallacy): An attempt to persuade through threat of harm. (*Chapter 6*)

Appeal to Ignorance (Fallacy): A fallacy in which, because something is not known to be true, it is assumed to be false; or, because it is not known to be false, it is assumed to be true. (*Chapter 6*)

Appeal to Pity (Fallacy): An attempt to persuade on grounds of compassion when compassion is not relevant to the argument. (*Chapter 6*)

Appeal to Popularity (Fallacy): A fallacy in which a claim is argued to be satisfactory on the grounds that it is widely believed to be true. (*Chapter 6*)

Appeal to Tradition (Fallacy): An assertion that because something has always been done a certain way, that way is correct. (*Chapter 6*)

Argument: A set of statements in which some statements (premises) are used to support another statement (the conclusion). (*Chapter 1*)

Argument from Analogy: An argument that draws a conclusion about one case (called the "primary subject") on the basis of its similarities to another case (called the "analogue"). (*Chapter 5*)

Begging the Question (Fallacy): A fallacy in which the truth of the conclusion is already assumed in the premises. (*Chapter 6*)

Categorical Logic: A subfield of formal logic that looks at the relationships between categories or groups. (*Chapter 7*)

Categorical Statement: A claim about whether the members of one category are, are not, or may be members of another category. (*Chapter 7*)

Categorical Syllogism: A form of argument in which one categorical statement is deduced from two other categorical statements. (*Chapter 7*)

Category: A group or collection of things. (*Chapter 7*)

Circular Definition: A definition in which a word that is included in the definiens is also part of the definiendum. (*Chapter 2*)

Circumstantial Ad Hominem (Fallacy): A fallacy in which an argument is rejected on the grounds that the arguer has some ulterior motive. (*Chapter 6*)

Common Knowledge: Any statement that is commonly known to be true. What constitutes "common knowledge" depends on the audience being addressed. (*Chapter 4*)

Complement: The opposite of a given category. For example, the complement of the category "eagles" is "non-eagles" (everything that is not an eagle). (*Chapter 7*)

Complex Argument: An argument that includes at least one sub-argument. (*Chapter 3*)

Complex Statement: A statement that includes more than one logical connective. (*Chapter 8*)

Component Statement: A statement that includes a logical connective and is embedded within a complex statement. (*Chapter 8*)

Composition Fallacy: A fallacy in which, because the parts of a whole have a certain property, it is assumed that the whole has that property. (*Chapter 6*)

Conclusion: The part of an argument that the premises are meant to demonstrate by means of evidence or justification. (*Chapter 1*)

Conclusion Indicator: A word or phrase that signals that a conclusion is being offered. (*Chapter 1*)

Conditional Statement: A statement of the form "If P, then Q." A conditional does not assert that P actually is the case but rather states that *if* P is the case *then* Q must be also. (*Chapter 8*)

Conjunction: A statement of the form "P and Q." A conjunction connects two other statements such that it is true if and only if the connected statements are true. For example, "Penguins are birds and dogs are mammals." (*Chapter 8*)

Connotation: Emotional or conceptual associations that are connected to a word but not part of its literal definition. (*Chapter 2*)

Consequent: The second proposition in an "If ..., then ..." conditional statement, immediately following the "then." In the conditional statement "If P, then Q," Q is the consequent. (*Chapter 8*)

Contradictories: Categorical statements in a pair such that if one is true, the other must be false, and vice versa. Statements of the A and O forms are contrary to one another; so are statements of the E and I forms. (*Chapter 7*)

Contraposition: A logical operation in which a categorical statement is converted (its subject and predicate are reversed) and "non-" is attached to both categories. (*Chapter 7*)

Contraries: Categorical statements that can both be false at the same time but cannot both be true at the same time. Statements of the A and E forms are contrary to one another. (*Chapter 7*)

Conversion: A logical operation performed on a categorical statement by switching the subject and the predicate. Only A and I statements can be converted while staying logically equivalent. (*Chapter 7*)

Conviction: The degree of confidence conveyed by a statement. (*Chapter 2*)

Counter-example: An example that refutes or contradicts a universal statement. (*Chapter 4*)

Deductive Argument: An argument in which the premises are intended to provide a guarantee of the truth of the conclusion. (*Chapter 5*)

Definiendum: In a definition, the word that is being defined. (*Chapter 2*)

Definiens: The definition of a word. (*Chapter 2*)

Definition by Example: A definition that appeals to examples of the definiendum in order to illustrate its denotation. (*Chapter 2*)

Denotation: What a word literally refers to. (*Chapter 2*)

Denying the Antecedent (Fallacy): Any argument of the following form: If A, then B. Not A. Thus, Not B. This argument form is always invalid. (*Chapter 6*)

Dependent Premises: Premises that work together to establish a conclusion (and so should be evaluated together). Removing one of the premises creates a logical gap. (*Chapter 3*)

Description: A statement or set of statements concerning how the world was, is, or will be. (*Chapter 1*)

Disjunction: A statement of the form "P or Q." A disjunction connects two other statements such that it is true if and only if one or both of the connected statements are true. For example, "Either penguins can fly or sparrows can fly." (*Chapter 8*)

Distribution: A property of categories within categorical statements. A category is distributed within a categorical statement if the statement indicates something about each and every member of that category. The subject category is distributed in A and E statements; the predicate category is distributed in E and O statements. (*Chapter 7*)

Division Fallacy: A fallacy in which, because the whole has a certain property, it is assumed that the parts have that property. (*Chapter 6*)

E Statement: A categorical statement of the form "No S are P." This states that no members of S are members of P. Also called a "universal negative." (*Chapter 7*)

Emotionally Charged Language: Language that conveys a strong positive or negative feeling or mood. (*Chapter 2*)

Equivocation (Fallacy): A fallacy in which the same term is used with two different meanings, but the argument treats both meanings as if they were the same. (*Chapter 6*)

Euphemism: A word or expression that is used in place of a more direct expression so as to avoid negative connotations. (*Chapter 2*)

Explanation: An attempt to show why some fact is true by appealing to contributing factors. (*Chapter 1*)

Factor: A fact or event that causes or influences another fact or event. (*Chapter 1*)

Fallacy: An intentional or unintentional error in reasoning. (*Chapter 6*)

False Dilemma (Fallacy): A fallacy in which two choices are given when in fact there are more options. (*Chapter 6*)

Faulty Analogy: An argument from analogy in which the primary subject and the analogue case have no similarities or only irrelevant similarities. (*Chapter 5*)

Faulty Analogy (Fallacy): A fallacy in which, in an argument by analogy, the two objects or events being compared have no relevant similarities or are relevantly dissimilar. (*Chapter 6*)

Group: See **Category**.

Guilt by Association (Fallacy): A fallacy in which a person's views are rejected because those views are associated with a group that is unpopular. (*Chapter 6*)

Hasty Generalization (Fallacy): A faulty generalization based on a sample that is unrepresentative or too small. (*Chapter 6*)

I Statement: A categorical statement of the form "Some S are P." This states that there exists at least one member of S that is also a member of P. Also called a "particular affirmative." (*Chapter 7*)

Improper Appeal to Authority (Fallacy): A fallacy in which an authority is invoked to provide support for the conclusion, but the authority is not an expert in the relevant area, or is not honest and reliable, or is not in agreement with other experts in this area, or the area is not something that one can be an authority about. (*Chapter 6*)

Inconsistency (Fallacy): A fallacy in which contrary or contradictory statements are asserted to be true at the same time. (*Chapter 6*)

Independent Premises: Premises that independently support the conclusion; each premise offers some degree of separate support for the truth of the conclusion. (*Chapter 3*)

Inductive Analogy: An argument by analogy in which the analogue must be a real case or group of cases. (*Chapter 5*)

Inductive Argument: An argument in which the premises are intended to provide a high degree of probability that the conclusion is true. (*Chapter 5*)

Intermediate Conclusion: A statement that is the conclusion of a sub-argument and is used as a premise for another conclusion within a complex argument. (*Chapter 3*)

Irrelevant Premise: A premise that is included in a given argument but has no bearing on whether the argument's conclusion should be accepted. (*Chapter 4*)

Logical Connective: A word or symbol that relates one statement to another or to itself. Not, and, v, and > are all logical connectives. (*Chapter 8*)

Logically Equivalent Statements: Statements that are true and false under the same conditions: meaning that they could both be true or both be false, but if one were true, the other could not be false. For example, "All S are P" is logically equivalent to "No S are not P." (*Chapter 7*)

Long Truth Table Method: The use of a chart to plot out all possible truth values of an argument's variables and statements in order to determine whether the argument is valid. If one or more rows in the table show the conclusion as false and all the premises as true, then the argument is invalid. (*Chapter 8*)

Main Conclusion: The foremost "idea" or "point" in an argument; the statement that the argument's premises and sub-arguments are ultimately meant to support. (*Chapter 3*)

Major Term: In a categorical syllogism, the predicate in the conclusion. (*Chapter 7*)

Middle Term: In a categorical syllogism, the term that appears in both premises but not the conclusion. (*Chapter 7*)

Minor Term: In a categorical syllogism, the subject of the conclusion. (*Chapter 7*)

Missing Premise or Conclusion: A premise or conclusion that is unstated but is required by the logical form of the argument. (*Chapter 3*)

Multi-vocal: Term applied to words that have more than one meaning. (*Chapter 2*)

Negation: A statement of the form "Not P." A negation is true if and only if the statement it negates is false. For example, "It is not the case that Vancouver is the largest city on Earth." (*Chapter 8*)

Negatively Relevant Premise: A premise that is included in a given argument and suggests that the argument's conclusion should not be accepted. (*Chapter 4*)

Neutral Language: Phrasing that does not carry positive or negative connotations. (*Chapter 2*)

O Statement: A categorical statement of the form "Some S are not P." This states that there exists at least one member of S that is not also a member of P. Also called a "particular negative." (*Chapter 7*)

Obscure Definition: A vague or difficult to understand definiens. (*Chapter 2*)

Obversion: A logical operation in which the scope of a categorical statement is switched (from positive to negative or from negative to positive) and "non-" is added to the predicate. All obverted statements are logically equivalent to their originals. (*Chapter 7*)

Ostensive Definition: A definition of a word given by a non-verbal action (as when you define the word "jump" by jumping) or by bringing someone's attention to the object the word refers to (as in pointing to a cat to define the word "cat"). (*Chapter 2*)

Particular Statement: A categorical statement that describes a property of some (but not all) members of the subject category. (*Chapter 7*)

Personal Testimony: A statement made by an individual about his or her own personal experience. Usually, personal testimony is satisfactory when the claim is plausible and the person is not known to be dishonest or unreliable. (*Chapter 4*)

Positively Relevant Premise: See **Supportive Premise**.

Post Hoc (Fallacy): A fallacy in which an arguer claims that since one event happened before another event, the first event must have caused the second. (*Chapter 6*)

Predicate Category: The group that is related to the subject category in a categorical statement. For example, in "All ants are insects," the predicate category is "insects." (*Chapter 7*)

Prejudicial Language: The use of biased terminology or vocal intonation to indicate or hint at personal feelings or opinions about the value, truth, or falsehood of the claim being made. (*Chapter 2*)

Premise: A reason that is used in an argument to support a conclusion. (*Chapter 1*)

Premise Indicator: A word or phrase that signals that there is a premise being offered. (*Chapter 1*)

Primary Subject: In an argument by analogy, the subject of the conclusion. (*Chapter 5*)

Problem of Induction: A problem with inductive reasoning about future events. The problem is that we can in general never be certain that future events will resemble past events, so no matter how many observations we've made about the past, we can't be certain that those observations will help us to accurately predict the future. Despite this problem, reasoning on the basis of strong inductive arguments is rational. (*Chapter 5*)

Propositional Logic: A type of symbolic logic that deals with the relationships between propositions using the basic logical connectives: 'and', 'or', 'not', and 'if ..., then'. (*Chapter 8*)

Qualified statement: A statement that does not convey certainty about what is true. Identified by such expressions as "It might be true that...." (*Chapter 2*)

Random Sample: A sample in which every member of the represented population has an equal prospect of being included. (*Chapter 5*)

Rational Persuasion: The use of an argument to cause another person to believe a conclusion. (*Chapter 1*)

Red Herring (Fallacy): A fallacy in which the arguer wanders from his or her argument to some other unrelated or tangential point, thereby distracting the audience. (*Chapter 6*)

Refute: To demonstrate that a statement is false. (*Chapter 2*)

Relevant Expert: An honest and reliable expert in a given area. A statement that is the shared opinion of relevant experts is usually satisfactory when used as a premise in an argument. (*Chapter 4*)

Relevant Premise: A premise that is included in a given argument (or sub-argument) and has bearing on whether the argument's conclusion should be accepted. (*Chapter 4*)

Reportive Definition: A dictionary-type definition that attempts to capture how a word is normally used. (*Chapter 2*)

Representative Sample: A sample that has the same distribution of all relevant characteristics as the whole population being considered. (*Chapter 5*)

Rhetorical Question: A question that has an implied answer and therefore functions as a statement. (*Chapter 1*)

Sample: A subset selection of a population. Samples are used for inductive generalizations. (*Chapter 5*)

Satisfactory Premise: A premise that is true or that there is good reason to believe is true. (*Chapter 3*)

Scope: The number or proportion of members of a group that a statement is referring to. A statement's scope may be narrow or broad. (*Chapter 2*)

Short Truth Table Method: A technique used in propositional logic to determine an argument's validity. In this technique, one begins by assigning the truth value of the conclusion to false and then filling in a table so as to determine whether the premises can all be true while the conclusion is false. If they can, then the argument is invalid. (*Chapter 8*)

Slippery Slope (Fallacy): A fallacy in which a series of increasingly unacceptable consequences are said to follow from an original position that appears to be acceptable. From this, it is claimed that the original position is therefore unsatisfactory. (*Chapter 6*)

Sound Argument: A deductive argument that is valid and has only true premises. (*Chapter 5*)

Square of Opposition: A graphic representation of the logical relationships between the four types of categorical statement. (*Chapter 7*)

Standardization: Rewriting of an argument by identifying and labelling its premises and conclusion(s). This is done in order to see the logical flow of the argument. (*Chapter 3*)

Statement: The expression of a single idea or concept; it can be either true or false. Also known as a "proposition" or a "claim." (*Chapter 1*)

S-Test: A means of evaluating an argument, according to which certain conditions must be met in order for the argument to be successful. These conditions are satisfactory premises that offer sufficient support for the conclusion. (*Chapter 3*)

Stipulative Definition: A definition whereby the speaker specifies how he or she is using a word, regardless of whether this conforms to normal use. (*Chapter 2*)

Straw Person Argument (Fallacy): A fallacy in which the arguer reconstructs an opponent's argument as something weaker than it actually is, then attacks that weaker version of the argument. (*Chapter 6*)

Strong Argument from Analogy: An argument from analogy in which the primary subject and the analogue case have relevant similarities and either no differences or only irrelevant differences. (*Chapter 5*)

Strong Inductive Argument: An inductive argument that successfully shows that its conclusion is highly likely. (*Chapter 5*)

Sub-argument: An argument provided to establish a statement that is then in turn used as a premise to justify another conclusion within a complex argument. (*Chapter 3*)

Sub-contraries: Categorical statements that can both be true at the same time but cannot both be false at the same time. Statements of the I and O forms are sub-contrary to one another. (*Chapter 7*)

Subject Category: The group that a categorical statement says something about. For example, in "All ants are insects," the subject category is "ants." (*Chapter 7*)

Successful Argument: An argument in which the premises are satisfactory and sufficiently support the conclusion. (*Chapter 4*)

Sufficiency of Support: When an argument's premises provide enough support for its conclusion such that, if its premises are satisfactory, acceptance of its conclusion is rational. (*Chapter 3*)

Supportive Premise: A premise that is included in a given argument and suggests that the argument's conclusion should be accepted. (*Chapter 3*)

Target Population: All individuals within the population that is being considered. For example, if you are attempting to determine the favourite book of Canadian school children, the target population is Canadian school children. (*Chapter 5*)

Truth Value: The truth or falsity of a statement. For example, the truth value of the statement "Ontario is a province of Canada" is "True." (*Chapter 8*)

Two Wrongs Make a Right (Fallacy): A fallacy in which a wrong action is defended on the basis that someone else did the same thing earlier. (*Chapter 6*)

Universal Statement: A categorical statement that describes a property of all members of the subject category. (*Chapter 7*)

Unqualified Statement: A statement that conveys certainty about what is true. For example, "It will definitely snow this weekend." (*Chapter 2*)

Unsupported Claim: A statement offered without any supporting evidence or argument. (*Chapter 1*)

Vagueness: When a word or sentence is so unclear that the listener cannot determine its specific meaning. (*Chapter 2*)

Valid Argument: A deductive argument in which the premises necessarily lead to the conclusion; that is, it is impossible for the argument's premises to be true AND its conclusion to be false. If it is possible for the premises of the deductive argument to be true AND the conclusion to be false, the argument is invalid. (*Chapter 5*)

Variable: A capital letter used in propositional logic to represent a proposition. (*Chapter 8*)

Venn Diagram: A diagram of overlapping circles representing a relationship between two or more categories. (*Chapter 7*)

Verbal Dispute: A disagreement about the meaning of a term. (*Chapter 2*)

Weak Argument From Analogy: An argument from analogy in which the primary subject and the analogue case have few relevant similarities or have relevant dissimilarities. (*Chapter 5*)

Weak Inductive Argument: An inductive argument that fails to show that its conclusion is highly likely. (*Chapter 5*)

Whole Argument: The entirety of premises and conclusions (including any sub-arguments) that make up an argument. (*Chapter 3*)

Index

From the Publisher

A name never says it all, but the word "Broadview" expresses a good deal
of the philosophy behind our company. We are open to a broad range of
academic approaches and political viewpoints. We pay attention to the
broad impact book publishing and book printing has in the wider world;
for some years now we have used 100% recycled paper for most titles.
Our publishing program is internationally oriented and broad-ranging.
Our individual titles often appeal to a broad readership too; many are
of interest as much to general readers as to academics and students.

Founded in 1985, Broadview remains a fully independent
company owned by its shareholders—not an imprint
or subsidiary of a larger multinational.

For the most accurate information on our books (including
information on pricing, editions, and formats) please
visit our website at www.broadviewpress.com. Our print
books and ebooks are available for sale on our site.

broadview press
www.broadviewpress.com